The Lutheran Course II
Leader Book

ABOUT "WINKING LUTHER(S)"

Martin Luther's theology is grounded in paradoxes—sinner/saint, law/gospel, hidden/revealed—and illuminated by a down-to-earth, everyday sense of humor. This icon of Luther winking at the reader combines the serious, formal scholarship that was his life's work with the humor and lightheartedness that characterized his personality.

The wink on Luther's face indicates that even though theology is serious stuff, we should nonetheless remember that it is not our theology that saves us, but Jesus Christ. Therefore, our life in the church can be buoyant, and our theological wranglings can be done with a sense of humor and love for our neighbor.

Because *The Lutheran Course II* takes after its predecessor, *The Lutheran Course*, in almost every way it is logical that "Winking Luther" should appear on the cover once again. Since it is a "sequel" of sorts, however, with 100 percent new content delivered in exactly the same style, a single "Winkie" would not do. Therefore, two identical Winking Luthers appear on the cover.

The Lutheran Course II

Leader Book

Augsburg Fortress
Minneapolis

THE LUTHERAN COURSE II
LEADER BOOK

Copyright © 2007 Augsburg Fortress. All rights reserved. Except for brief quotations in critical articles or reviews, no part of this book may be reproduced in any manner without prior written permission from the publisher. Write to: Permissions, Augsburg Fortress, Box 1209, Minneapolis, MN 55440.

Scripture quotations are from New Revised Standard Version Bible, copyright, 1989 Division of Christian Education of the National Council of the Churches of Christ in the United States of America. Used by permission. All rights reserved.

Quotation from the Augsburg Confession, Article 18, in Session 2 is from page 50 of *The Book of Concord*, ed. Robert Kolb and Timothy J. Wengert, © 2000 Augsburg Fortress. All rights reserved.

Hymns marked ELW are from *Evangelical Lutheran Worship,* Augsburg Fortress, 2006.

Quotations from *Luther's Works (LW),* volumes 32, 27, and 6, are copyright © Fortress Press 1972, 1964, and 1970 (respectively). The volume number appears first; the page numbers follow.

Editors: Laurie J. Hanson and Josh Messner
Writer: Hans Wiersma
Cover Art: Spunk Design Machine
Interior Art: Brenda Brown

ISBN 978-0-8066-6069-1

Also available:
The Lutheran Course II Course DVD
ISBN-13: 978-0-8066-6070-7

The Lutheran Course II Workbook
ISBN-13: 978-0-8066-6068-4

The Lutheran Course II Promo Pack
ISBN-13: 978-0-8066-6071-4

The Lutheran Course II Starter Kit
ISBN-13: 978-0-8066-6067-7

The Lutheran Handbook II
ISBN-13: 978-0-8066-7037-9

The paper used in this publication meets the minimum requirements of American National Standard for Information Sciences—Permanence of Paper for Printed Library Materials, ANSI Z329.48-1984.

Manufactured in the U.S.A.

10 09 08 07   1 2 3 4 5 6 7 8 9 10

CONTENTS

Introduction	7
Setting Up *The Lutheran Course II*	10
Your Role as the Large Group Leader	22
Session 1 How to Tell the Difference between Theology of the Cross and Theology of Glory (How does God work?)	28
Session 2 How to Tell If Your Will Is in Bondage to Sin and What to Do about It (Why do we do things we know we shouldn't do?)	37
Session 3 How to Receive God's Grace Daily (How are we saved?)	46
Session 4 How to Tell the Difference between a Sinner and a Saint (If we're saved, why do we still sin?)	53
Session 5 How to Identify a "Neighbor" and What This Means for Lutherans (If we're saved, can we do whatever we want?)	60
Session 6 How to Tell the Difference between the Kingdom on the Left and the Kingdom on the Right (Should Christians be involved in the world?)	67
Session 7 How to Tell the Difference between a "Vocation" and a "Vacation" (Can we make a difference in this world?)	75
Course Overview	83
Small Group Leader's Guide	84
Table Talk Pages	87
Course Evaluation Form	96

INTRODUCTION

A Family Reunion

The Lutheran Course II works something like a family reunion, except no one needs to bring a camera, pose for pictures, or say, "Cheese." Like a family reunion, there will be an arrival time, a gathering of the whole family, conversations in smaller groups, farewells, and the ride home.

Table Talk

Martin Luther shared a great deal of wisdom and practical advice in informal conversations over dinner, a tradition known as "Table Talk." And in honor of that tradition, this course invites people to come to the table to talk and learn.

As participants arrive for each session of the course (or at each meal, if this course is taking place during a retreat), they will be invited to enjoy a time of informal Table Talk. This portion of the session is very much like the exciting moments right after you arrive at a family reunion— when you eagerly catch up on the lives of your relatives, celebrating successes and enjoying each other's company. It's in that same spirit of love and sharing that participants in *The Lutheran Course II* will gather for each session, catching up with old friends, making some new friends, and sharing what's been going on in their lives.

Large Group Stuff

The session then shifts focus to hearing and learning with the entire large group. This is like that special time in a family reunion when everyone settles back and shares stories. In *The Lutheran Course II*, this happens with a video that follows a narrator as he talks with people on the street, Lutheran scholars, and congregations.

Small Group Stuff

Participants are then invited to move into small groups for more intimate and focused conversations. This part of the session looks like the fun interludes that happen during a family reunion when smaller groups of siblings or cousins run off to their favorite spots to talk. So in *The Lutheran Course II*, small groups of six to eight adults meet in separate areas for more focused discussion on the session's topic.

Wrap-Up

Next, everyone reconvenes in the large group. This is much like the good-byes families say at the end of a reunion. In *The Lutheran Course II*, each session wraps up with a litany and a blessing.

At-Home Stuff

But that's not the end of the session, because participants will find themselves continuing their reflections and conversations about these topics on the drive home and into the following days. (If you are using a retreat format for the course, invite participants to try out some At-Home Stuff between sessions.)

The Adventure Begins

Before you set out on this exciting adventure, it's a good idea to know what pitfalls to avoid. As in any adventure, there are dangers—occupational hazards, if you will—for the leaders of both the large group and the small group. The first and greatest is the temptation to have the definitive answer, the final word, or the great truth. While you do need to have answers to things such as what the schedule looks like and who is in charge of certain tasks, you by no means need to have definitive answers on other matters. That's because most adults learn best when they have a chance to think and talk and pray about questions that perplex them, and then come to answers that will work best for them.

The second danger in leading this course, or really any course, is that somehow, without warning, this whole process will mutate into something predictable and dull. That means that the times of refreshment and song, the times of large-group presentation and small-group discussions will somehow lose their freshness and turn stale. And the quickest way to slide down the hill into a dry routine is to take the course, or any of the activities, too seriously. One sure way to strip away the energy and excitement about the course is to get caught up in worrying about "getting it right" instead of enjoying the moments of joyful sharing, laughter, and insight. So to prevent this from happening to you, approach each session as a time of *celebration* for participants to come and be refreshed. And leave the concerns about "getting it right" at the door.

So relax, have fun. Come to the reunion. Eat a little, sing a little, laugh a whole lot. Enjoy yourself and enjoy the company of the participants in *The Lutheran Course II*.

Showing the world you're a Lutheran can be accomplished in part by means of a bumper sticker, but this should not represent the totality of your faith expression.

SETTING UP
THE LUTHERAN COURSE II

If you are reading this section of the book, you have probably agreed to serve as the large group leader for *The Lutheran Course II*. Congratulations! You have taken on an important and exciting role! Now it is time to make all of the needed preparations to ensure that this course runs smoothly.

This section of the *Leader Book* is designed to help you with the "big picture," which includes the planning and organization of the course. If you have led courses before, you are probably familiar with many of the steps we will go over in the next few pages. If you are new to the responsibilities involved in leading a course, then you will want to pay particular attention to these important foundational steps, since each one will contribute to the success of the course.

Laying the Foundation

The success of any congregational event lies in building a solid foundation. The foundation for *The Lutheran Course II* needs to be strong and sturdy. Two key ingredients make up a strong and sturdy foundation for this course. The first ingredient is prayer—prayer for God's wisdom as you lead this course and God's blessings for every facet of the course as it unfolds. The second ingredient is collaboration—a spirit of mutual cooperation and service between those running the course and your congregation's leadership and ministry teams.

The Foundation of Prayer

The first step in leading this course is to ask God to guide you. That's because the responsibility for leading a course on Lutheran theology and how it relates to daily life requires God's wisdom. And try as you might, you will only be spinning your wheels if God isn't leading your every step. Psalm 127:1 reads, "Unless the Lord builds the house, those who build it labor in vain. Unless the Lord guards the city, the guard keeps watch in vain." So it's a great idea to begin planning this course with prayer and to continue to ask for God's leading and blessing each step of the way.

The Foundation of Leadership

Through prayer, the groundwork for the course is already being established. But for the foundation to be strong and sturdy, it must be dug deeply into the soil of the congregation and anchored securely to the congregation's leadership. Therefore, you will want to meet with the pastor(s) in your congregation to ensure you have support for going ahead and offering *The Lutheran Course II* to the congregation. (If you are the pastor, or if you have been recruited by the pastor for this duty, you can skip this step.)

Then the next step in building a strong and sturdy foundation for the course is to gain the support of the congregational ministry teams serving in the areas of adult education. Consider giving a brief overview of the course to the council and church ministry teams and invite their feedback and support. This step is valuable, not only because it informs key church leaders about the course, but because it gives everyone in a leadership position a chance to weigh in on the course. It also gives you a chance to entertain useful feedback while answering any questions or concerns that are raised. More important, it gets people talking about the course well before any of the publicity goes out. This early step of foundation-building plants seeds of excitement about the course throughout the congregation, and those seeds will yield a full harvest when the course is ready to run.

Skillfully Scheduling

Using a Session Format

The Lutheran Course II can be offered to your congregation in a number of formats. Since the course is organized into seven sessions, ideally, you will be able to offer the course over seven weeks, beginning each session with a meal followed by approximately a 90-minute time slot for the course material itself. The course could be scheduled into your Sunday morning education time. Should this option work best for your congregation, we suggest that you double the number of course sessions to 14. See table 1 for more detailed information on how to use seven or 14 sessions for the course.

Table 1. Session planning guide

Note: Time for each session component is given in minutes.

Total Session Length	Table Talk	Opening	Video Presentation	Large Group Activity	Small Group Stuff	Wrap-Up
2½ hours	40	20	20	10	50	10
2 hours*	30	15	20	5	40	10
1½ hours	15	10	20	5	35	5
1 hour Week One	15	15	20	10	Skip until next session	
1 hour Week Two	Pick up from previous session			10	40	10
45 min. Week One	5	10	20	10	Skip until next session	
45 min. Week Two	Pick up from previous session			5	35	5

*The ideal session length would be at least two hours.

Using a Retreat Format

Another option is to present the course in a retreat format. A retreat might fit into some participants' schedules more easily than seven or 14 separate sessions. A retreat setting also allows participants to get away from home and their usual routines so they can focus on the course. See table 2 for a sample schedule using a retreat format, and feel free to revise this schedule to suit your group and the retreat facilities.

Table 2. Sample schedule for a retreat

Note: Time for each session component is given in minutes.

	Opening	Video Presentation	Large Group Activity	Small Group Stuff	Wrap-Up
Friday					
Supper* 5:30–6:30 P.M.					
Session 1 6:30–7:40	15	20	5	25	5
Session 2 8:00–9:00	5	20	5	25	5

*Option: Use Table Talk questions from the *Leader Book* during one or all of the meals.

Sample schedule continued on next page.

Sample schedule continued.

Table 2. Sample schedule for a retreat

Note: Time for each session component is given in minutes.

	Opening	Video Presentation	Large Group Activity	Small Group Stuff	Wrap-Up
Saturday					
Breakfast* 8:00–8:30 A.M.					
Session 3 8:30–9:40	15	20	5	25	5
Session 4 10:00–11:00	5	20	5	25	5
Lunch* 11:30–12:30 P.M.					
Session 5 1:00–2:00	5	20	5	25	5
Session 6 2:30–3:30	5	20	5	25	5
Session 7 4:00–5:00	5	20	5	25	5

*Option: Use Table Talk questions from the *Leader Book* during one or all of the meals.

Consider Child Care Needs

Whether you choose to present *The Lutheran Course II* in seven sessions, 14 sessions, or a weekend retreat, consider making arrangements for child care to make it easier for parents with young children to participate in the course.

Avoid Scheduling Conflicts

People in our society are busy and oftentimes over-scheduled. So as you set the dates and times for *The Lutheran Course II*, avoid as many known scheduling conflicts as possible. Check the larger church calendar early on to make sure this course won't conflict with other key events that have already been planned. You may also want to check with the local school calendars for upcoming concert dates, athletic events, and other activities that parents and grandparents plan to attend. And you may even want to consult with the TV listings to find the days/times of popular shows and professional sports events that will draw people away from attending. Now, you can't avoid all scheduling conflicts. But getting a lay of the land will help ensure greater success for the course.

Reserve Adequate Space

Choosing and reserving adequate space for *The Lutheran Course II* is just as important as scheduling. Take time to do this now so you can welcome your group to a comfortable space free of distractions. Also set aside adequate space for child care, if needed.

Table Talk

Should you be following the recommended format for each session in the course, you will first need to reserve a place for the course participants to gather, to share a meal or refreshments, and to engage in informal Table Talk. This space could be a fellowship hall or large classroom with a kitchen facility nearby.

Large Group Stuff
The opening, video presentation, and large group activity may occur in the same space where the group has gathered, or you may want to consider moving the group to some other location where you have a video system available.

Small Group Stuff
Following the large group presentation, participants will form smaller groups of six to eight people. Separate spaces for each group can enhance sharing and support privacy. Should you go this route, be sure to reserve smaller rooms for each session. If individual rooms are not available, then you can create space for these small groups within the larger room by assigning areas/tables for each group to use during this section of the course.

Wrap-Up
Reconvene the large group for the closing litany and sending. Whatever location you choose for this, be sure to reserve it for each session.

Helpful Planning Sessions

As you move into the planning and preparation phase of this course, you may find it helpful to assemble a team to assist you in planning and running the course. Be sure to write into your schedule the times and dates when you and your team will meet to plan and organize this course, and then be sure to reserve the space you need for these meetings.

Finally, this course has been designed to incorporate small group leaders as facilitators for the small group discussions. Schedule a time to meet with the small group leaders a week or so before the course begins so you can equip them for their role.

The Team

Many people can be involved in planning this course and running it effectively. Listed below are some key roles that will help make this course a blessing for all who participate.

Publicist

Distributing course information to the congregation and the community is one of the most important roles in preparing for this course. And it is good to supply this information through a number of channels and for at least six to eight weeks prior to the start of the course itself. Use the church newsletter as well as the posters, bulletin inserts, and promo videos in the Promo Pack, or use e-mail, message boards, the church Web site, and bulletin boards to let folks know what the course is all about. This can help people make an informed decision about attending. Taking the time to send personal invitations to adults in your congregation can create greater interest and participation.

Then you will want to think about the process and time frame that adults will need to follow in order to sign up for the course. If you have an interactive Web site, registration could take place online. Another option would be to have people call the church office to sign up for the course. Whatever you decide, it is important to have a cutoff date about a week before the course begins. That will help you with your final course planning. But we all know that you will probably get last-minute stragglers signing up for the course. So it's important to be flexible as you make plans for the initial large group gathering and refreshments, and as you form the small groups and assign the small group leaders, so you can incorporate any latecomers with ease.

We recommend that you follow these three easy steps to promote *The Lutheran Course II*:
1. Be sure to let everyone know that this course is for adults, Lutheran or not. Prospective church members and other friends in your community might enjoy the course as much as lifelong Lutherans.
2. Begin advertising *The Lutheran Course II* to your potential audience at least six weeks in advance—two months is better.
3. Use all available communication channels with the adults in your congregation (bulletins, newsletters, verbal announcements during worship, and so on). Also use the bulletin inserts, posters, and promo videos for the course, which are available in *The Lutheran Course II Promo Pack* (ISBN-13: 978-0-8066-6071-4).

Musician(s)

Each session of the course will include an opportunity for worship and song. To enhance the worship experience, it is important to recruit the most gifted person, or the best ensemble, that you can. And as you guide these musicians in providing music for this course, help them understand that you want the singing to be filled with life and enthusiasm.

This course will provide you with music suggestions for each session, with recommendations from *Evangelical Lutheran Worship* (*ELW*; Augsburg Fortress, 2006). Please note that musicians should not feel restricted to these suggestions. Having a combination of the gift of music, a good sense of humor, and a great sense of energy and worship will allow your musician(s) to bring a powerful element to each of your course sessions.

Table Talk Coordinator

You probably know someone in your congregation who just loves to throw a party. When you look around, you can most likely think of some folks who seem to naturally light up when they are in charge of hosting any size reception or celebration. Now, this is not really a surprise to us, since God has given individuals in the body of

Christ various gifts and talents. And although the gift of hospitality is not one listed in 1 Corinthians 12, it is a precious gift often found within the church. And finding someone with this gift to handle the Table Talk portion of the sessions will set the stage for a great time! That's because the opening Table Talk section of the session usually involves food—a whole meal if you can work that out, or at least dessert or maybe some light refreshments. And the opening Table Talk section of each session is built on an atmosphere of celebration, good conversation, and some pleasant surprises. Suggestions for how to set up the opening Table Talk portion of each session, and recommendations on how to get the conversation started, are included in this *Leader Book*. A person who is truly gifted with hospitality and who has awareness of and sensitivity to the theme and message of each session can flawlessly and creatively launch each session.

Small Groups and Small Group Leaders

Since each session of the course includes both large and small group activities, the number of course participants you have will impact your planning and organization of the sessions. Therefore, as participants sign up, it's a very good idea to prayerfully assign them to small groups of six to eight participants. It is good to balance each small group with a cross section of ages and situations, along with common interests and experiences, to provide the most fertile ground for the small group experience. When you are assigning people to small groups, remember that your primary goal is to create groups in which members trust each other enough to share their thoughts and feelings openly so they can learn from each other.

You also should recruit one small group leader for each group that you form. Select your small group leaders with care since they will have a profound impact on the success of the groups they lead. Small group leaders do not need to have formal theological training or team building experience. But they should possess a loving attitude toward others, have the ability to understand and appreciate diverse ideas, have good personal boundaries, have the presence to guide conversation in a spirit of exploration and discovery, and be gregarious enough to start a conversation and keep it going. Your small group leaders have an important role to play in the overall success of this course—and that is to facilitate discussions that are helpful and supportive.

Finding gifted people to lead the small group discussion can seem like a difficult task. And it is. But it is important to avoid the temptation to put more than eight people in a group just so that you don't need to recruit so many small group leaders. When a small group isn't small anymore, the group leader's job becomes much more difficult, and participants won't get as much out of the course. Small groups should be small enough that everyone will feel comfortable speaking up. Remember, small group leaders don't need to be experts. So inviting people who can effectively facilitate these small group discussions can be an exciting adventure for you and your congregation, as more and more people have a chance to grow in using their God-given gifts!

Team Training

One thing that will help you recruit small group leaders is your promise to train them in all that they will need to know. This means meeting with them prior to the first session so that you can walk through the Small Group Leader's Guide. This meeting may be the only training they need. But many of your small group leaders may feel better if you meet several times through the course, and a few may even wish to meet prior to every session. You know your small group leaders best (after all, you recruited them), so determine how frequently you will need to meet together.

Plan to include the following in your small group leader's training meeting:

- Hand out copies of *The Lutheran Handbook II* (Augsburg Fortress, 2007) to each leader so he or she can read it over and become familiar with its purpose and tone.

- Hand out copies of the *Workbook* and explain what parts are used in the large group, what parts are used in the small group, and what parts are used by participants at home.

- Outline the components of a typical session, with particular attention paid to the small group segment.

- Distribute and review copies of the Small Group Leader's Guide (pp. 84–86 in this *Leader Book*).

- Give a sneak preview of the course by showing the promo videos (ISBN-13: 978-0-8066-6071-4).

- Answer any questions small group leaders may have about their roles and responsibilities.

- Demonstrate how to begin the first small group meeting by facilitating introductions and informal sharing and by going over the Small Group Covenant (p. 7 in the *Workbook*).

- Try to include several fun role plays in your training session to give your small group leaders a chance to practice group facilitation skills. You may want to have one role play focused on handling silence and another one addressing a small group member who always wants to be right, for example.

- Take time to celebrate the launching of the course with a festive meal or light refreshments. This serves as a wonderful way to let your small group leaders know how much you appreciate their willingness to minister with you in the weeks ahead.

Materials and preparation
Finally, you will need to order a sufficient number of copies of *The Lutheran Handbook II* and *The Lutheran Course II Workbook* so that they will arrive in time for the first session.

YOUR ROLE AS THE LARGE GROUP LEADER

This *Leader Book* and the course *Workbook* contain a wide range of tools to help you fulfill your role as the large group leader and course coordinator. The course material is organized into seven sessions with each session divided into four sections: Table Talk, Large Group Stuff, Small Group Stuff, and At-Home Stuff. As you read over both resources, please feel free to select only those tools that will work best for you and for your setting.

Table Talk

The informal sharing time that begins each session is called Table Talk. It's named after the sort of informal conversation Martin and Katie Luther shared with their students and guests around their own table at the old Augustinian cloister at Wittenberg. In the Table Talk section of each session, you will be given suggestions on how to prepare the actual space where participants will convene so they can easily talk together and have fun as they focus on things related to the session. As you implement these recommendations, feel free to be creative and add touches that will fit your setting.

The reproducible pages at the back of the *Leader Book* will help you prepare the Table Talk portion of your sessions. If you are incorporating a potluck or another type of meal, you may need to plan a half hour or more for the Table Talk period. If you have decided to offer just some light refreshments, then you might plan for about 20 minutes. But if it's dessert you're serving, be sure to give everyone the chance to savor each delicious morsel before moving on!

Large Group Stuff

As you move into the large group portion of the session, you will serve as the host. That means you will be responsible for organizing and supervising all that happens during the large group section so things run smoothly.

Refer to the Overview for each session well in advance of the session itself. You'll find the Overview at the start of each session in the *Leader Book* and the *Workbook*. It's designed to help you and the participants gather information about the central theme and the major points that will be covered in that session.

The Opening

After people move from the Table Talk section of the session into the space for Large Group Stuff, start with the Opening and some lively Lutheran singing. The Opening section of each session will include some song and hymn suggestions. However, you are free to incorporate whatever songs, hymns, or choruses you think will best tie in with

Don't hesitate to delegate. If you don't actively hand over authority and responsibility to your team, you might get saddled with all of it!

the theme of the session while fitting your own church setting. Feel free to select lively music that will help your participants move into a spirit of worship and praise.

The Opening will also include a Scripture reading and prayer. Invite team members or course participants to take turns reading the scripture and offering the prayers each time you meet. To keep the course moving forward, it is recommended that you plan up to 20 minutes for the Opening section of the course. As always, please be flexible in light of your own setting and the needs of your participants.

The Video

Introduce the speaker, topic, and video for the session. It is important to have the video presentation cued and ready to go as soon as the introduction has concluded. That means you will probably want to test all of the equipment and cue the DVD before anyone arrives for the session. And in setting up the audiovisual equipment, it's important to use a screen large enough for everyone to see. Also, check the sound quality before each session to make sure it is loud enough and clear enough for everyone to hear.

Large Group Activity

The *Workbook* is provided to help participants focus their attention on specific information covered in each session. The Large Group Stuff section is designed for use before and after the video presentation. As the large group leader, you are free to pick and choose from the activities offered in the *Workbook* to best reinforce the points made by the video. And as you facilitate the large group discussion, be sure to pay attention so that all who would like to share can have a chance. But be mindful of the clock, remembering that everyone will have more opportunities to share within the small groups.

If you are conducting *The Lutheran Course II* on Sunday mornings, or in some other limited time frame in which you are splitting each session over two weeks, then plan on ending the first week of a topic with the Large Group Stuff section. Then when you pick up the course the next week, you can start with these very same pages as a way to review the material you covered the previous week. Also, please note that there are some Large Group Stuff activities that are best suited for use right after the video presentation during the first week of a session topic. And there are other activities that would be more appropriate to use the second week of a topic, as a way to review the material from the first week before the participants move into small groups.

An effective way to mark the ending of the Large Group Stuff and the transition to the Small Group Stuff (or to mark the ending of the session if you are using a 14-week format) is with a song. Consider incorporating an appropriate song at this juncture to help bring the Large Group Stuff to a close.

Small Group Stuff

The session now moves into Small Group Stuff, a time for small groups of six to eight people to gather for conversation. The first time you meet, it will be very important for you to give participants clear instructions about which group they have been assigned to and where their group is meeting. As efficient as you have been in planning for the small group sessions, assigning people to small groups, training the small group leaders, and getting the rooms/spaces for small group discussions set up and ready, during the first session of the course you will be asked to tend to a wide variety of needs and questions as folks begin to move into their small groups. Plan on being available for whatever comes your way. Also, once people have settled into their small groups, you may want to check in with each group to make sure everyone is comfortable. And then the small groups should be left to accomplish the work before them. Catch your breath for a minute or two while you collect your thoughts and offer prayers that the participants will gain new insights into Lutheran theology and their daily lives.

Wrap-Up

Participants generally emerge from their small groups with energy and enthusiasm. As you gather feedback from several or all of the small groups, encourage positive and enriching information that will not violate confidences of the small groups. And if the groups are quiet (which is unlikely), ask about a specific Small Group Stuff question or return to the Large Group Stuff section of the *Workbook* to generate some closing discussion.

Lead the litany for the session and have participants join you in the response. And yes, there's always time for one more song.

At-Home Stuff

The questions and activities in At-Home Stuff give participants suggestions for continuing to explore the session topic on their own. As the large group leader, encourage them to use these suggestions. Then ask them to read the selected pages from *The Lutheran Handbook II*, as these pages will lead right into the next session.

Summary of Each Session

Table Talk

Invite participants to use these ideas and discussion starters as they gather.

Large Group Stuff

Opening: Sing songs, read Scripture, and pray together.

Video: Introduce the video presentation.

Workbook: Use the Large Group Stuff pages of the *Workbook* to reinforce the video.

Small Group Stuff

Small group leaders and participants use the Small Group Stuff pages of the *Workbook* to spark discussion.

Wrap-Up

End the session with brief discussion and a closing litany.

Evaluation

At the end of Session 7, ask participants to fill out the Course Evaluation Form (p. 96). Review this feedback to find out what went well and what could be improved. Then consider offering the course again. Some of those who just finished the course might be willing and available to help with this.

HOW TO TELL THE DIFFERENCE BETWEEN THEOLOGY OF THE CROSS AND THEOLOGY OF GLORY (How does God work?)

Overview

Objective
The first session introduces the biblical (and Lutheran) concept of a "theology of the cross" (*theologia cruces* in Latin) and contrasts it with a "theology of glory."

Materials needed
○ name tags
○ Table Talk cards for Session 1
○ songbooks
○ a Bible
○ *The Lutheran Handbook II*
○ *The Lutheran Course II Workbook*
○ Course DVD
○ DVD player and screen
○ DVD of *Indiana Jones and the Last Crusade* (optional)

Jesus of Nazareth was not the only person crucified in the first century. Crucifixion was a favored form of capital punishment in the days of the early Roman Empire. However, Christians ever since have insisted there is something special about the cross of Jesus, since it is through this cross that God has chosen to be revealed. You can do a lot of things with the cross of Christ: wear it around your neck, tattoo it on your bicep, sign it over your chest, put it on your steeple, and even sew it into your flag (as in many European flags).

You can say a lot of things about the cross of Christ as well. Martin Luther stated the matter simply: "The CROSS alone is our theology" (*Weimarer Ausgabe* 5:176). The fact that Luther wrote the word *cross* in capital letters emphasizes that he wanted to emphasize the emphasis on the cross! (Or to put it another way, Luther believed the main thing was to make the main thing the main thing.) Luther was simply taking his cue from the apostle Paul, who once declared, "I decided to know nothing among you except Jesus Christ, and him crucified" (1 Corinthians 2:2). While some Christians will insist that there's got to be more to it than "just" the cross, other Christians—especially Lutherans—will insist that the cross is the be all and end all of Christ's work among us on earth.

28   The Lutheran Course II

Table Talk

Participants will discuss these questions as they arrive:
- Think of words or terms that contain the word *cross* (for instance, *cross section* or *crossed fingers*). How many can you name?
- Name one thing you could brag about, if you were the bragging type.
- Why do you think the legendary vampire Dracula is kept at bay by holding up a cross?
- How do you define the word *theologian*?

Suggest that one person at each table pick up a Table Talk card at random, respond to the question, and pass the card to the person to the right, who will also answer the question and pass the card on. When that card has gone around the table, someone else can pick up another card and repeat the process until time is up.

Large Group Stuff

Opening

Welcome participants and introduce yourself. If appropriate for the size of the group, invite a few participants to share examples of their responses to the Table Talk questions. Next, give a brief overview of *The Lutheran Course II*. For example: "In this course, we will look at key themes of Lutheran Christianity, for instance, faith versus works, saint versus sinner, even vacation versus vocation. From these examples, you can see that Lutheran Christians like to think in terms of opposites. The first opposites we'll look at are two conflicting theologies: 'theology of glory' versus 'theology of the cross.'"

Read or have a participant read the Overview on page 8 of the *Workbook*.

Session 1

Session preparation
○ Read the session material in this *Leader Book*, the *Workbook*, and the *Handbook*.
○ Preview the entire DVD presentation.
○ Set up DVD player and screen.
○ Cue DVD.
○ Set up refreshments.

Table Talk preparation
○ Make copies of the Table Talk cards on page 87.
○ Cut on the dotted lines.
○ Place a set of four cards on each table.

The Lutheran Handbook II readings for this session:
pp. 161–63, 170–73, 191–92, 283
(The First Article: On Creation)

Hymn suggestions

Each of these hymns speaks of the admittedly odd idea of glorying in nothing else but the cross of Christ.
- *ELW* 324
- *ELW* 335
- *ELW* 338

Invite a participant to read the key scripture text for this session: "May I never boast of anything except the cross of our Lord Jesus Christ" (Galatians 6:14). Explain that the writer of the verse, the apostle Paul, could have bragged about any number of things: how much faith he had, how much religious training he'd received, how much he'd suffered for the sake of Jesus, and so on. Instead, he insisted that the only thing worth bragging about was the work and wisdom of Christ on the cross. Invite someone to read 1 Corinthians 1:17–31 for more explanation of what Paul means when he speaks of boasting in the cross alone. Explain that while various theologies of glory seem sensible by human standards, a theology of the cross insists that God's work will not be subject to human standards.

Introduce the opening prayer with the following exchange:

    Leader: **The Lord be with you.**
    Group: And also with you.
    Leader: **Let us pray.** . . .

Merciful God, your Son was lifted up on the cross to draw all people to himself. In the cross, you reveal yourself to us under the sign of the opposite. Foolish, weak, and despised, your cross brings to nothing our human ideas of wisdom, power, and glory. Give us, therefore, eyes to see and ears to hear; through Jesus Christ, your Son, our Lord. Amen.

Video

Introduce the video: The video presentations for *The Lutheran Course II* follow a narrator, Bryan McInnis, as he learns about key opposites or paradoxes in Lutheran Christianity and what they mean for daily life. For each session, McInnis travels to a different location to talk with people on the street, a Lutheran scholar, and members of a Lutheran congregation. For this session on theology of the cross and theology of glory, our narrator travels to Philadelphia, Pennsylvania, to speak with Timothy J. Wengert, Ministerium of Pennsylvania Professor, Reformation History, The Lutheran Theological Seminary at Philadelphia; and members of Trinity Evangelical Lutheran Church, Lansdale, Pennsylvania.

Play the Session 1 DVD presentation in its entirety. After the presentation, ask for any initial reactions. (Receive all responses.) Which person in the video was most intriguing? Why?

The cross is key to salvation and the way God works.

Large Group Activity

❶ The Christian claim that God is particularly known in the crucified Jesus is counterintuitive to say the least. Two thousand years of Christianity have perhaps dulled us to the preposterousness of the original claim: "For God so loved the world that he gave his only Son" (John 3:16). This large group activity is designed to get participants thinking about the divine wisdom hidden in the foolishness of the cross. Some ancient graffiti provides a lead-in to this subject.

Direct participants to turn to page 9 in the *Workbook*, the page with the "Alexamenos Graffito." Provide participants with the following information:
- The "Alexamenos Graffito," carved on the wall of the ruins of a boys' school in Rome, was discovered in 1857.
- Most scholars believe that the graffito is authentic and dates to a time before A.D. 300.
- Today, you can see the graffito for yourself at the Palatine Antiquarium Museum in Rome.
- Written in Greek (a language that would have been taught to boys attending this school), the caption translates: "Alexamenos worships [his] God."

This drawing, called the "Alexamenos Graffito," is a good place to begin our investigation of various understandings (or theologies) of the cross. The Greek inscription translates: "Alexamenos worships [his] God."

Ask participants what they see in the crude drawing. (The drawing features two figures. The central figure is a crucified man with the head of a donkey. To the left is a figure (supposedly Alexamenos) with his hand extended in reverence of the figure on the cross.) Explain to participants that in the Roman world, there were many gods and goddesses. What bothered many people about Christians was not only that they worshiped a crucified God, but also that they stubbornly refused to worship all other gods. Bowing down to a God who was executed in cruel Roman fashion seemed dumb enough; insisting that the crucified God was the *only* God worthy of worship seemed even worse—an idea deserving of severe mockery (if not worse). Hence the cartoon making fun of poor ol' Alexamenos.

To introduce your group to the idea of the divide between a theology of the cross and various theologies of glory, lead them in the following activity.
1. Form two groups, A and B.
2. Invite those in Group A to think of or write down two or three reasons why they might understand that the message of the cross reveals God to the world.
3. Invite those in Group B to write down two or three reasons why they might understand that the message of the cross reveals only weakness and foolishness.
4. Invite participants on both sides to share their responses with the large group.

Afterward, note how in most cases the reasons given by Group B have to do with human expectations and standards for divine behavior.

❷ If there is time, read the items listed under "How to Tell the Difference between Theology of the Cross and Theology of Glory," beginning on page 170 of *The Lutheran Handbook II*. Be prepared to get things started by providing some examples of theology of the cross and theologies of glory. Ask participants to respond to these items with their comments or questions. Don't feel that you need to have answers for all of their questions. Being a theologian of the cross is not something that one learns in a one-hour session; it is something that one becomes at the hands of the Crucified and Risen One.

Multimedia Option

As mentioned in *The Lutheran Handbook II* (p. 171), "once you start looking for theologies of glory you begin to see them everywhere." One fine example of a theology of glory is found in the movie *Indiana Jones and the Last Crusade* (1989; PG-13). In the climactic scene, Indy must solve a series of booby-trapped puzzles to reach the Holy Grail. Before he can obtain the "Cup of the Carpenter," he has to "prove his worth" by (1) bowing in penance, (2) following in the footsteps of God's proper name, (3) taking a leap of faith, and (4) selecting the true grail from dozens of false ones. This represents a typical theology of glory: God's salvation—in this case, the healing cup—can only be attained by proper human decision and effort. On the other hand, there is a subtle theology of the cross in this scene as well. When it comes to selecting the real cup of Jesus out of all of the fake ones, Indy ignores all of the chalices made of gold and jewels and opts instead for the humblest goblet.

Start DVD at 1:43:45 (just before Indy attempts the first puzzle); stop DVD at 1:54:10 (as Indy leaves the chamber with the grail). Give participants an opportunity to identify the theology of glory and the theology of the cross demonstrated in this scene.

Small Group Stuff

Direct participants into small groups to discuss the questions on page 10 in the *Workbook*. Tell the groups what time to return for Wrap-Up. Be ready to answer questions as needed.

Wrap-Up

Review small group discussions by having participants from each group respond to one or more of the following questions:

- What are some of the more interesting crosses you have seen?
- What are some typical human expectations of God?
- What is the most difficult aspect of "understanding" the cross of Christ?

Conclude with words like these: "Lutherans have preferred to think of the cross of Jesus as the place where God is revealed 'hidden under the opposite' (or, if you want to impress your friends with Latin: *deus absconditus sub contrario*). For Lutherans, speculation about what God might be like, in all of God's glory, is discouraged. Knowing God is not achieved by accessing some trove of secret knowledge or through transcending human existence. Instead, for Lutherans, there is a stubborn insistence that God has chosen to be known through the crucified and risen Son, Jesus Christ."

The Bible is filled with examples of unlikely people assisting God's mission. In this case, Pharaoh's daughter adopts Moses, a Hebrew baby, as her son, saving him from certain death.

As a follow-up to the theme of this session, invite participants to spend the days ahead listening for everyday talk that reflects a theology of glory or a theology of the cross. Ask them to return next time ready to share examples. Also in preparation for the next session, invite participants to read the related material in *The Lutheran Handbook II*.

Closing Litany and Prayer

Lead, or invite a participant to lead, the following responsive prayer based on "Jesus, Keep Me Near the Cross" (*ELW* 335; text by Fanny L. Crosby, 1820–1915).

Leader: The Lord be with you.
Group: And also with you.
Leader: Let us pray. Jesus, keep us near the cross, where there is a precious fountain of life, free to all.
Group: In the cross, let my glory be forever, for there my ransomed soul will be at rest.
Leader: Near the cross, where love and mercy find trembling souls, and light shines all around.
Group: In the cross, let my glory be forever, for there my ransomed soul will be at rest.
Leader: Near the cross, and in its shadow, help us live from day to day.
Group: In the cross, let my glory be forever, for there my ransomed soul will be at rest.
Leader: Near the cross, make us watch and wait, hope and trust, until we reach the heavenly shore.
Group: In the cross, let my glory be forever, for there my ransomed soul will be at rest.
Leader: Remember us in your kingdom, O Lord, and teach us to pray: "Our Father . . . *[finish with the Lord's Prayer]*."

HOW TO TELL IF YOUR WILL IS IN BONDAGE TO SIN AND WHAT TO DO ABOUT IT (Why do we do things we know we shouldn't do?)

Overview
• • • • • •

Lutheran Christianity does not put any confidence in "free will" when it comes to being saved by God. The original Lutheran confession of faith spells this out plainly: "Without the grace, help, and operation of the Holy Spirit a human being cannot become pleasing to God, fear or believe in God with the whole heart, or expel innate evil lusts from the heart" (Augsburg Confession, Article 18). In other words, our relationship with God is broken and there's nothing we can do to fix it. We are bound—bound to choose against the good, bound to choose against God. Of course, if our choice is bound, then it's really no choice at all.

The sense that all humans are by nature inclined (bound!) to choose against God is behind the idea of "original sin." "All have sinned and fall short of the glory of God" (Romans 3:23) is how the apostle Paul famously described the human condition. The human heart is "curved in on itself," more often motivated by self-interest than by self-sacrifice. As Paul observed in himself, "I see in my members another law at war with the law of my mind, making me captive to the law of sin that dwells in my members. Wretched man that I am! Who will rescue me from this body of death?" (Romans 7:23-24). When we're stuck, we're stuck. We can't *will* ourselves to be unstuck. Instead, we need someone to come and get us unstuck: "Thanks be to God through Jesus Christ our Lord!" (Romans 7:25).

Session 2

Objective
This session will investigate "freedom of choice" in light of the notion that humans are *bound* to choose what they want rather than what God wants.

Materials needed
- name tags
- Table Talk cards for Session 2
- songbooks
- a Bible
- *The Lutheran Handbook II*
- *The Lutheran Course II Workbook*
- pens or pencils
- Course DVD
- DVD player and screen
- newspapers
- magazines
- DVD of *Groundhog Day* (optional)

Session preparation
○ Read the session material in this *Leader Book*, the *Workbook*, and the *Handbook*.
○ Preview the entire DVD presentation.
○ Set up DVD player and screen.
○ Cue DVD.
○ Set up refreshments.

Confessing in public that your will is bound to sin and that you cannot free yourself will help reorient you toward the One whose will is not bound to sin and who can, in fact, free you.

Table Talk

Table Talk preparation
○ Make copies of the Table Talk cards on page 88.
○ Cut on the dotted lines.
○ Place a set of four cards on each table.

Participants will discuss these questions as they arrive:
- What (if anything) did you choose to have for breakfast this morning? *Why* did you choose this?
- Form a sentence using the word *will* at least three times (for example, "What will Will will to Will Jr.?" or "Your will will will differently than my will will will").
- List some things you did not choose (when you were born, where you were born, to whom you were born, your DNA, your kindergarten teacher, that broken arm in eighth grade, falling in love, and so forth).
- In five words or less, define *sin*.

Suggest that one person at each table pick up a Table Talk card at random, respond to the question, and pass the card to the person to the right, who will also answer the question and pass the card on. When that card has gone around the table, someone else can pick up another card and repeat the process until time is up.

Session 2

Large Group Stuff

Opening

Welcome participants to this, the second session of *The Lutheran Course II*. Welcome any newcomers, reintroduce yourself, and, if appropriate to the size of the group, invite participants to reintroduce themselves. Ask for examples of theology of glory and theology of the cross that participants have noted since the last session. Next, invite a few participants to share responses to the Table Talk items for this session.

Hymn suggestions
Note that the last hymn, based on Psalm 130, was written by Martin Luther. Hymns about sin and repentance tend to have a medieval feel about them, perhaps because sin and repentance are not very popular themes in the modern world.
- *ELW* 600
- *ELW* 604
- *ELW* 606

Offer a brief introduction to the theme of this session: "Last time we took a look at two conflicting theologies: 'theology of glory' versus 'theology of the cross.' Today, we will consider another set of ideas that are difficult to reconcile: the 'free will' and the 'bound will.'"

Read or have a participant read the Overview on page 12 of the *Workbook*.

Invite a participant to read the key scripture text for this session: "For I do not do the good I want, but the evil I do not want is what I do" (Romans 7:19). Explain that the writer of the verse, the apostle Paul, was probably the least likely person to make such an admission. Under the Law of Moses, Paul understood that he was "blameless" (Philippians 3:6). Yet under the crucified and risen Christ, Paul recognized that he was the foremost sinner (1 Timothy 1:15). Many of us can relate to Paul's confession regarding good intentions and bad conduct. Paul observed that when it comes to producing results, the human will falls short.

The Lutheran Handbook II readings for this session:
pp. 29–31, 42–45, 178–80, 184–85, 280–82

Introduce the opening prayer, based on Psalm 51:1, 2, 10, with the following exchange:

Leader: The Lord be with you.
Group: And also with you.
Leader: Let us pray. . . .

Have mercy upon us, O God, according to your steadfast love. In your great compassion, blot out our offenses. Wash us from wickedness through and through, and cleanse us from sin. Create in us clean hearts, O God, and renew a right spirit within each of us; through Jesus Christ, your Son, our Lord. Amen.

Video

Introduce the video: For this session on free will and bound will, our narrator travels to the LaCrosse, Wisconsin, area to speak with April Ulring Larson, bishop, LaCrosse Area Synod; and members of Coon Valley Lutheran Church in Coon Valley.

Play the Session 2 DVD presentation in its entirety. After the presentation, ask for any initial reactions. (Receive all responses.) Which person in the video was most intriguing? Why?

Because we are bound to sin, we need constant confession and forgiveness.

Large Group Activity

❶ Direct participants to turn to page 13 in the *Workbook*. To introduce the activity, offer these words (or something like them): "To explore the topic of human sin, we're going to take a look at the news. Grab a newspaper and/or magazine." (These can be distributed or participants may retrieve them from a central stack.) "Look for stories that provide examples of behaviors that are the result of bad—perhaps even evil—choices. Pick one or two stories and read the headlines aloud to the group."

After various headlines have been read, say: "Let's take a vote to see which story (or stories) the whole group is interested in exploring further." Ask the participant(s) who chose the winning story or stories to read aloud the most essential facts.

With the group, analyze the story in light of the following questions (these questions are also printed in the *Workbook*):
1. What is the bad (or downright evil) choice behind the conduct described in this news story?
2. What law (human and/or divine) has been violated in this story?
3. What thought process might have led to the bad choice?
4. What thoughts, words, and/or deeds from the story demonstrate that humans are "curved in on themselves"?

In a news story about a man arrested for bank robbery, you might respond to the four questions like this: (1) The man chose to attempt taking money from a bank. (2) This is against both criminal law and the commandment, "You shall not steal." (3) The man thought he needed money; he thought he could get away with it; he thought the bank had plenty of money. (4) He didn't think about how his crime would affect others; he didn't consider the consequences of getting caught; although the robber probably would agree that stealing is wrong, especially if someone stole from him, he didn't think the rule against stealing applied to him.

Large group preparation
○ Write each of the following approaches to conflict on a separate piece of poster board or newsprint:
  • Avoid
  • Accommodate
  • Compete
  • Compromise
  • Collaborate
○ Place the five posters around the room, with space between them for people to gather.

❷ Ask participants to think of bad choices they have made (whether recently or in the distant past). Analyze these choices with the same questions used to analyze the news stories. Then ask this question: "In which ways were you 'bound' to make the choices you made?" (Participants should not be asked to share the particulars of their former sins. However, it may prove fruitful for a participant to share a reflection about "bondage" to a particular choice.)

Optional: If there is time, check out these entries in *The Lutheran Handbook II*: "How to Tell If Your Will Is in Bondage to Sin and What to Do about It" (pp. 178–80) and "How to Tell the Difference between Original Sin and Everyday Sin" (pp. 184–85). The first entry reinforces this lesson; the second entry provides helpful additional material in regard to the relationship between "original sin" (that innate tendency to disobey God, what medieval theologians called *concupiscence*) and everyday run-of-the-mill sins. How did the DVD presentation deal with these issues?

Multimedia Option

One symptom of being captive to sin is that "you find it easy to neglect the needs of others in favor of your own needs" (*The Lutheran Handbook II*, p. 178). This symptom describes weatherman Phil Conners in the movie *Groundhog Day* (1993; PG). In this film, the self-absorbed, self-centered, and selfish Phil (Bill Murray) finds himself reliving the same day over and over again. It's not just déjà vu; instead, Phil is stuck (bound?) in a cycle in which he wakes up at 6:00 a.m. on February 2 day after day after day. Furthermore, the cycle seems designed to make Phil despair of his own self-centeredness. Indeed, it is only when Phil finally is driven to true selflessness that he is released to experience February 3! In this clip, Phil is experiencing Groundhog Day for the third day in a row. At day's end, he realizes his actions will have no consequences. His realization proves true when he wakes up in his hotel room on Groundhog Day again, despite being thrown in jail the night before. The clip is a fine representation of how someone "curved in on himself" might actually live if he discovered he really could do whatever he wanted. *"Bon appétit,"* Phil is told.

Start the DVD at 0:29:44 (with Phil in the bowling alley); stop the DVD at 0:37:58 (after Rita says, *"Bon appétit"*). If you continue with the scenes beyond *"Bon appétit,"* you will see just how low Phil will stoop to satisfy his appetites.

Questions to ask:
- What would you do if your actions had no lasting effects? Would you live a more moral life, or would you throw your morals to the wind?
- What does it say about us that we need rules and the threat of consequences to keep our desires and conduct in check?

Small Group Stuff

Direct participants into small groups to discuss the questions on page 14 in the *Workbook*. Tell the groups what time to return for Wrap-Up. Be ready to answer questions as needed.

Wrap-Up

Invite participants to bring their small group discussions to a close. In the large group, ask participants to share examples of their responses to the small group discussion questions. To wrap up, invite responses to the following questions. Of special interest might be participants' definitions of *addiction* and responses to the Luther quotation, "God's will is done only if yours is not done."

- How much free will does a two-year-old have? What kinds of boundaries do parents put around the exercise of their child's will?
- Is it possible that God puts boundaries around the exercise of the human will as well?

Let participants know that the theme of a bound will—the notion that our choice is less free than we like to think it is—is a key theme of Lutheran Christians because it is a key theme for the New Testament. The picture painted in the New Testament is of a human race stuck in the consequences of sin—its "bent-ness" toward self and away from God. The good news of the New Testament is that God sends Jesus to rescue, to save. In fact, the very name *Jesus* ("Y'shua" in Hebrew) means "God rescues" or "God saves." If all that was needed to save us was for us to exercise free will a bit more effectively, then God would have sent an encourager, a motivator, or perhaps a life coach. Instead, God sends a rescuer, a Savior—one who sets bound humans free. There will be more on this in the next session.

As a follow-up to the theme of this session, invite partpcipants to look for ways humans are captive to sin and to come to the next session prepared to share examples. Also encourage participants to read the related material in *The Lutheran Handbook II*.

Session 2

Closing Litany and Prayer

To close, lead the following responsive reading/prayer based on Psalm 130.

> **Leader:** The Lord be with you.
> Group: And also with you.
> **Leader:** Let us pray. We cry to you, O God, from the depth of our being. If you kept track of all our sin, who could stand?
> Group: We wait for you, O Lord.
> **Leader:** But with you there is forgiveness, O Lord.
> Group: We wait for you, O Lord.
> **Leader:** With you there is hope.
> Group: We wait for you, O Lord.
> **Leader:** With you there is steadfast love and a new, abundant life.
> Group: We wait for you, O Lord.
> **Leader:** For you, O God, will redeem your people from their sin.
> Group: We wait for you, O Lord.
> **Leader:** Remember us in your kingdom, O Lord, and teach us to pray . . .
> *All: Our Father . . . [lead the group in your preferred form of the Lord's Prayer] . . . Amen.*

HOW TO RECEIVE GOD'S GRACE DAILY (How are we saved?)

Objective
This session presents the core Lutheran idea—that we are justified by God's grace through faith apart from works of the law—in such a way that faith is not made into a new work of the law.

Materials needed
- name tags
- Table Talk cards for Session 3
- copies of the Session 3 Skit (pp. 90–91)
- songbooks
- a Bible
- *The Lutheran Handbook II*
- *The Lutheran Course II Workbook*
- pens or pencils
- Course DVD
- DVD player and screen
- DVD of *Shrek* (optional)

Overview

Can you think of anything wrong with the idea that salvation is not something you choose, but something God chooses for you? (This was the final question in last session's Small Group Stuff.) The answer is: *Yes! Of course there's something wrong with this idea! Because if my salvation is God's choice, it means I am not in control of my destiny.* A God who takes our destiny out of our hands, however, is a God who loves us—and the rest of the world—so much "that he gave his only Son, so that everyone who believes in him may not perish but may have eternal life." That's John 3:16, of course, and it's the gospel in a nutshell.

Humans curved in on themselves cannot work their way into divine favor by doing a prescribed amount of good works, subscribing to the correct religious doctrine, or mustering up enough belief in that doctrine. *Everyone falls short!* So God sent Jesus, the divine Son, to do the work for us and rescue us from our predicament. By joining us to the crucified and risen body of Christ, God takes control of our eternal destiny. God does this by grace, through faith, apart from good works. Here, in a nutshell, is how the apostle Paul put it: "We hold that a person is justified by faith apart from works prescribed by the law" (Romans 3:28). And again in Ephesians 2:8-9: "For by grace you have been saved through faith, and this is not your own doing; it is the gift of God—not the result of works, so that no one may boast." And God lets you know you have been saved by giving you *faith*.

The Lutheran Handbook II readings for this session:
pp. 88–90, 136–38, 148–50, 283–84 (The Second Article: On Redemption), 296

Table Talk

Participants will discuss these questions as they arrive:
- Is there such a thing as a free lunch?
- What is the most gracious thing someone did to (or for) you this past week? What is the most gracious thing you did for someone else (if you don't say so yourself)?
- Grace. Forgiveness. Faith. Promise. Hope. Love. Charity. Rebirth. Which of these are nice names for a baby? Which are basic biblical concepts?
- Name somebody you know who has a strong faith.

Suggest that one person at each table pick up a Table Talk card at random, respond to the question, and pass the card to the person to the right, who will also answer the question and pass the card on. When that card has gone around the table, someone else can pick up another card and repeat the process until time is up.

Large Group Stuff

Opening

Welcome participants and review the last session. To follow up on the previous session, ask for examples of ways that humans are captive to sin. Next, invite responses to the Table Talk items for this session.

Give a brief introduction to the session. For example: "In the last session, we discussed free will and bound will. Wills in bondage to sin cannot choose God's will. But this bondage is not the last word. God's amazing grace sets us free from our bondage to sin and death and brings us new life."

Read or have a participant read the Overview on page 16 of the *Workbook*.

Session preparation
- Read the session material in this *Leader Book*, the *Workbook*, and the *Handbook*.
- Preview the entire DVD presentation.
- Set up DVD player and screen.
- Cue DVD.
- Set up refreshments.

Table Talk preparation
- Make copies of the Table Talk cards on page 89.
- Cut on the dotted lines.
- Place a set of four cards on each table.

Hymn suggestions

Some of the greatest hymns center on God's amazing grace granted to us through faith in Jesus Christ.
- *ELW 623*
- *ELW 759*
- *ELW 779*
- *ELW 781*
- *ELW 796*
- *ELW 807*

Invite a participant to read the key scripture text for this session: "If the Son makes you free, you will be free indeed" (John 8:36). Explain: "These are the words of Jesus. He is speaking about being set free from sin and its consequences. It's possible that Jesus could have said, 'If you do enough good works, you will be free indeed,' or 'If you can work up enough sincere faith, you will be free indeed,' or even 'If you accept the fact that I have set you free, you will be free indeed.' Instead, Jesus makes clear that he himself sets humans free from sin." As Luther himself confessed: "God has taken my salvation out of my hands into his, making it depend on his choice and not mine, and has promised to save me, not by my own work or exertion but by his grace and mercy. . . . This is how all the saints glory in their God" (*Luther's Works* 33:289). Luther's statement is, of course, a sincere expression of faith. But his faith is the *result* of the freedom granted him by Christ, not the cause of it.

Introduce the opening prayer (Prayer for Fifth Sunday in Lent, Year A, *ELW*, p. 28) with the following exchange:
Leader: The Lord be with you.
 Group: And also with you.
Leader: Let us pray. . . .

Almighty God, your Son came into the world to free us all from sin and death. Breathe upon us the power of your Spirit, that we may be raised to new life in Christ and serve you in righteousness all our days, through Jesus Christ, our Savior and Lord, who lives and reigns with you and the Holy Spirit, one God, now and forever. Amen.

Video

Introduce the video: For this session on God's grace, our narrator travels to Atlanta, Georgia, to speak with Lawrence J. Clark, executive director, Lutheran Theological Center in Atlanta; and members of Lutheran Church of the Redeemer.

Play the Session 3 DVD presentation in its entirety. After the presentation, ask for any initial reactions. (Receive all responses.) Which person in the video was most intriguing? Why?

Session 3

Large Group Activity

❶ Give copies of the skit printed on pages 90–91 to four volunteers and invite them to act out the parts. The skit intends to demonstrate how faith (that is, trust) is the result of (rather than the cause of) parental grace and love. This is the preferred way to understand the gift of faith. After the skit, invite participants to reflect on the manner in which trust is formed in their own relationships. Ask: "Is there a difference between the trust a child might have for a parent and the trust an adult might have for a friend or a spouse?"

❷ Invite participants to share their responses to the statement "Faith is . . ." on page 17 of the *Workbook*. Facilitate discussion, pointing back to the skit as needed. You might make these comments in reference to the choices in the *Workbook*.
   a. Many people see faith as just another good work, but faith results from God's grace. It doesn't cause it.
   b. Faith is a gift, not something we muster up.
   c. God doesn't give us salvation in exchange for faith. God gives salvation because of God's amazing grace.
   d. This is Luther's classic understanding of faith. Faith results when God's gracious Word is communicated to us in Word and Sacrament.

Multimedia Option

To illustrate the idea that faith is the consequence of salvation, rather than the other way around, consider the rescue scene in the first *Shrek* movie (2001; PG). In this scene, the ogre Shrek has come to save Princess Fiona from her prison in the castle tower. Fiona has certain ideas regarding how and by whom she should be rescued; she prefers to be saved on her terms instead of on Shrek's terms. Even after Shrek successfully rescues her from captivity, Fiona continues to resist her savior because he does not meet expectations. It is not until later in the movie—as Fiona comes to know and appreciate Shrek—that her faith (trust) in Shrek begins to take shape.

Please note:
The first printing of *The Lutheran Handbook II* contained errors in the entry "How to Receive God's Grace Daily" on page 136. The first bullet point should read, "Don't do anything. Receiving God's grace doesn't depend on what you do or how much you believe. Grace can only be received as a free gift from God through Jesus Christ."

Start the DVD at 0:35:10 (where Shrek has arrived in Princess Fiona's prison chamber); stop the DVD at 0:43:45 (where Fiona, clutched by her rescuer, Shrek, begins to resign herself to the fact of her liberation). Caution: The clip contains a joke about Shrek's donkey, which uses a synonym for the word *donkey*.

Questions to ask:
- Why does Princess Fiona resist her rescuer?
- Why does Shrek *not* wait until the princess trusts him (accepts him) before he liberates her?
- In this rather ungracious scene, is there anything that illustrates the concept of *grace*?
- What is the meaning of this Bible passage: "While we were enemies, we were reconciled to God through the death of his Son" (Romans 5:10)?

Small Group Stuff

Direct participants into small groups to discuss the questions on page 18 in the *Workbook*. Tell the groups what time to return for Wrap-Up. Be ready to answer questions as needed.

Wrap-Up

Invite participants to bring their small group discussions to a close. In the large group, ask participants to share examples of their responses to the small group discussion questions. To wrap up, invite responses to the following questions:

- *Justification* is not a word we use every day. Or is it? How is *justification* used in regard to formatting text on a page? (In word processing there's *left justify, center justify, right justify, full justify*, or "This sentence is *justified* with the left margin.") How does the idea of being "properly aligned" relate to the idea of being "justified" by God?
- Lutheran Christians claim that the teaching about "justification by grace through faith" is "the article by which the church stands or falls" (in Latin, *articulus stantis et cadentis ecclesiae*). Why is this teaching so important?

As a follow-up to the theme of this session, invite participants to reflect on trust and relationships and to return next time with examples of grace. Also encourage participants to read the related material in *The Lutheran Handbook II*.

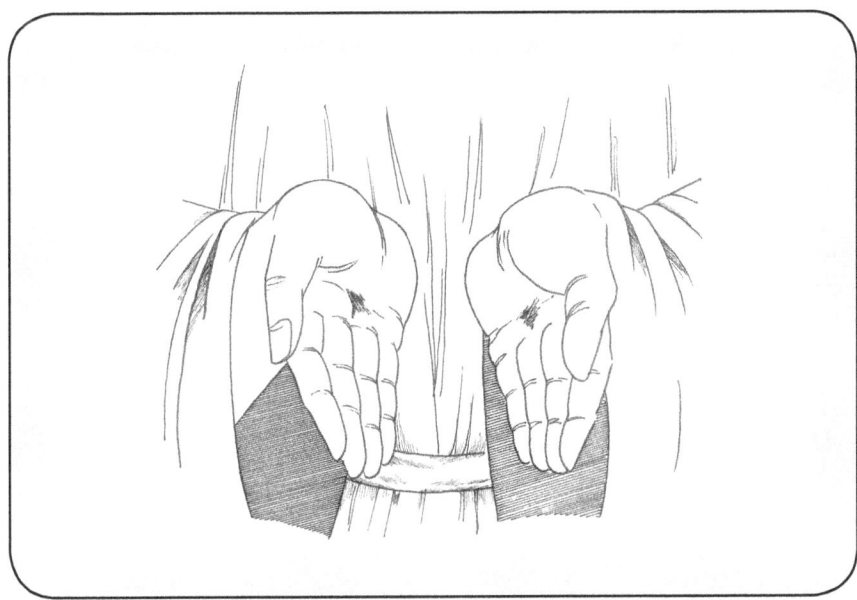

Jesus' blood and innocent suffering and death paid for our sins. This is costly grace.

Closing Litany and Prayer

Leader: The Lord be with you.
Group: And also with you.
Leader: Let us pray. Gracious Lord, your Word declares that while we were your enemies we were reconciled to you through the death of your Son. [Romans 5:10]
Group: Your Son has set us free, O God; we are free indeed.
Leader: Gracious Lord, your Word declares that since we are justified by faith, we have peace with you through our Lord Jesus Christ. [Romans 5:1]
Group: Your Son has set us free, O God; we are free indeed.
Leader: Gracious Lord, your Word declares that it is by grace we have been saved through faith, and that this is not our own doing but your gracious gift. [Ephesians 2:8]
Group: Your Son has set us free, O God; we are free indeed.
Leader: Gracious Lord, your Word declares that for freedom, Christ has set us free. [Galatians 5:1]
Group: Your Son has set us free, O God; we are free indeed.
Leader: Remember us in your kingdom, O Lord, and teach us to pray . . .
All: Our Father . . . *[lead the group in your preferred form of the Lord's Prayer]* . . . Amen.

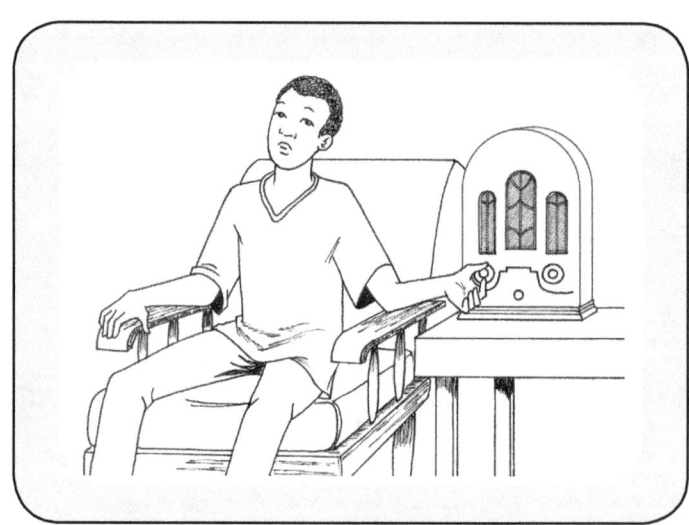

God's grace comes to us as a free gift.

HOW TO TELL THE DIFFERENCE BETWEEN A SINNER AND A SAINT (If we're saved, why do we still sin?)

Session 4

Objective
This session will illustrate the Lutheran concept that a Christian is both saint and sinner at the same time, demonstrating the tension between righteousness and sin within each believer.

Overview
• • • • • •

Lutherans love "two-handed" thinking. For example, on the one hand, you've got *theology of glory*, *free will*, and *justification by works*. On the other hand, you've got *theology of the cross*, *bound will*, and *justification by faith*. Luther and Lutherans didn't make up this kind of thinking, of course. You'll find such thinking in the New Testament, especially in Paul's letters. Nowhere is two-handed thinking more pronounced than in the understanding of a Christian person. Put simply, a Christian is two persons rolled into one! On the one hand, a Christian, though saved, is still sinful by nature: disobeying God's commands, disbelieving God's Word, and, consequently, dying. On the other hand, joined to Christ's body, the Christian shares Christ's attributes: obedience, faithfulness, and everlasting life—to name but a few.

In the New Testament, there are a number of different ways that these two "personalities" are described: flesh and spirit, old nature and new nature, old self and new self. Whichever way you slice it, the New Testament portrays the believer as righteous and sinful all at once (or here comes the Latin again, *simul iustus et peccator*). And although we might wish the church was full of saints, or even expect it to be, we know that's not the case. The church is made up of believers—believers who are saints and sinners at the same time!

Materials needed
○ name tags
○ Table Talk cards for Session 4
○ songbooks
○ a Bible
○ a piece of chocolate
○ signs or poster boards with the *Jeopardy!*-style answer-and-question items written on them (optional)
○ *The Lutheran Handbook II*
○ *The Lutheran Course II Workbook*
○ pens or pencils
○ Course DVD
○ DVD player and screen
○ DVD of *Chocolat* (optional)

The Lutheran Handbook II readings for this session: pp. 151–52, 186–87, 268–69, 284 (The Third Article: On Being Made Holy)

Table Talk

Session preparation
- Read the session material in this *Leader Book*, the *Workbook*, and the *Handbook*.
- Preview the entire DVD presentation.
- Set up DVD player and screen.
- Cue DVD.
- Set up refreshments.

Participants will discuss these questions as they arrive:
- Which of the Ten Commandments do you think is easiest to keep? (You'll find the Commandments in Exodus 20 and Deuteronomy 5.)
- How many of the Ten Commandments are also written into criminal law where you live?
- In 10 words or less, define *hypocrisy*. Next, give an example of hypocrisy.
- What does it mean to have a "left brain" and a "right brain"? What does it mean to be "of two minds"?

Suggest that one person at each table pick up a Table Talk card at random, respond to the question, and pass the card to the person to the right, who will also answer the question and pass the card on. When that card has gone around the table, someone else can pick up another card and repeat the process until time is up.

Table Talk preparation
- Make copies of the Table Talk cards on page 92.
- Cut on the dotted lines.
- Place a set of four cards on each table.

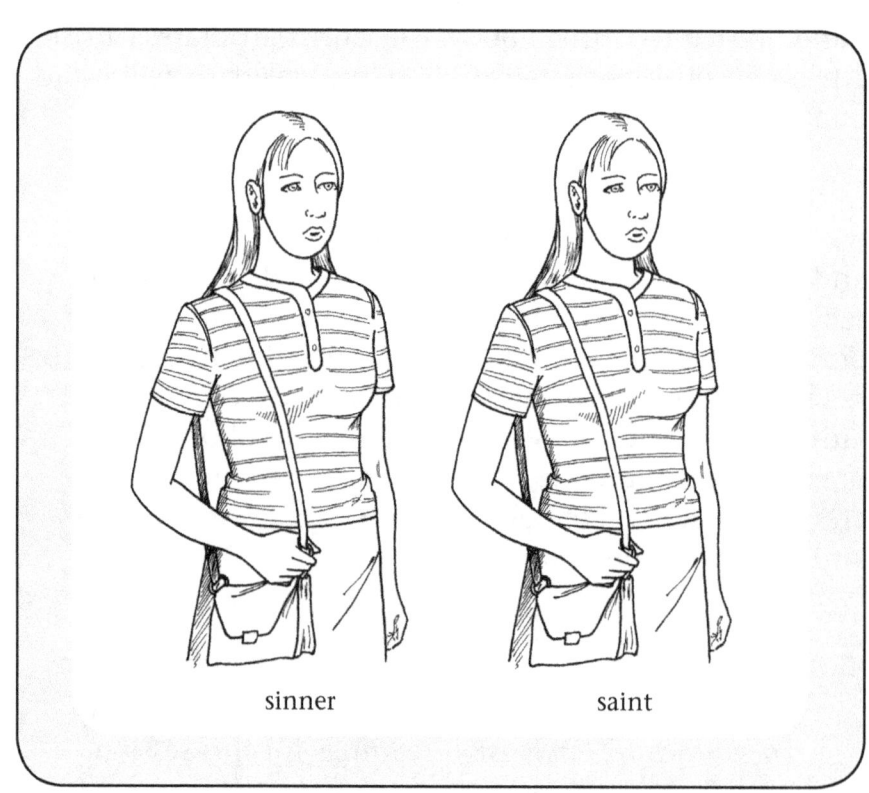

It's impossible to tell a sinner from a saint, because all people are fully both. The church is filled with them.

54 The Lutheran Course II

Large Group Stuff

Opening

Welcome participants and review the last session. Ask for examples of grace that participants have noted since the previous session. Next, invite responses to the Table Talk items for this session.

Give a brief introduction to the session. For example: "Mahatma Ghandi reportedly once said, 'I like your Christ. I do not like your Christians. They are so unlike your Christ.' Christians, though saved, are nevertheless not always very saintly. In this session we will explore the Lutheran (and biblical) contention that Christians are righteous and sinful—saints and sinners—at the same time."

Read or have a participant read the Overview on page 20 of the *Workbook*.

Invite a participant to read the key scripture text for this session: "What is born of the flesh is flesh, and what is born of the Spirit is spirit" (John 3:6). Jesus said this while talking to a religious leader named Nicodemus. Jesus had already told this leader that he must be "born from above." Nicodemus objected that he couldn't physically be born a second time. But Jesus countered that to see the kingdom of God, you must be "born of water and Spirit" (John 3:5). Rebirth in Christ leads to a unique earthly existence for a believer. The believer must live out this earthly life as a dual personality of sorts: an old creature and a new creation—a sinner and a saint—wrapped up in one body.

Introduce the opening prayer with the following exchange:
  Leader: The Lord be with you.
   Group: And also with you.
  Leader: Let us pray. . . .

Most merciful God, we are captive to sin and cannot free ourselves. We have sinned against you in thought, word, and deed, by what we have done and what we have left undone. And yet you forgive us, renew us, and lead us. Therefore, we give you thanks, that you are able to love sinners and make them into saints, through Jesus Christ, your Son, our Lord. Amen.

Hymn suggestions
The following represent some of the hymns that remind us that we are *sinners* in need of a Savior *and* that we are *saints* because of that Savior.
- *ELW* 325
- *ELW* 369
- *ELW* 606
- *ELW* 609
- *ELW* 631
- *ELW* 742

Video

Introduce the video: For this session our narrator travels to Berkeley, California, to speak with Martha E. Stortz, professor of historical theology and ethics, and Jane E. Strohl, associate professor of church history and Reformation history, Pacific Lutheran Theological Seminary; and members of Shepherd of the Hills Lutheran Church, Berkeley, California.

Play the Session 4 DVD presentation in its entirety. After the presentation, ask for any initial reactions. (Receive all responses.) Which person in the video was most intriguing? Why?

Large Group Activity

❶ Direct participants to the large group activity for this lesson (on p. 21 of the *Workbook*). Select volunteers to bring the three temptation situations to life. One person will be the "Temptee." Another person will be the angel, seated at the right of the Temptee; a third person will be the little devil, seated on the left. You can use a different group of three people for each of the vignettes. Have the piece of chocolate and a pencil ready for the Temptee to use. Then let the angel and the devil go at it, each one encouraging, cajoling, and persuading the Temptee toward the desired outcome.

This exercise will work best if you set a time limit of one or two minutes for each temptation. If the Temptee has not caved in when time is up, the little angel wins. If the Temptee does cave, the little devil wins.

After the entire exercise is ended, discuss it with participants. Is this a useful way to think about what takes place in the human conscience? What was persuasive about the devil's words? What was persuasive about the angel's words?

❷ In the TV game show *Jeopardy!* contestants are given the answers and, in turn, must give the corresponding question. The *Jeopardy!*-style items below are based on material in the session overview and/or in "How to Tell the Difference between a Sinner and a Saint" in *The Lutheran Handbook II* pp. 186–87. You may simply read the answers and invite group members to offer their responses. But remember, responses must be submitted in the form of a question. (Example: The answer is: *You can't.* The question is: *How can you tell the difference between a saint and a sinner?*)

To make this activity somewhat authentic, prepare a board with the answer-and-question items. You can do this using sheets of paper and a chalkboard, a dry-erase board, or a flip board. Write the *questions* directly onto the board. Next, over each question, tape a piece of paper with the *answer* written on it. Finally, for maximum effect, over each piece of paper, tape another piece of paper with a dollar value ($100, $200, $500, and so forth). This will allow participants to choose the answer they want by saying, for example, "Saints and Sinners for $200." If you want, you can provide extras such as "Double Jeopardy" under one of the items or "Final Jeopardy" for the last item. Invite three volunteers to be "official" contestants.

Category: "Saints and Sinners"

The answer:	Correct response (in question form):
A preferred way of thinking among Lutherans.	What is two-handed thinking?
A prerequisite for being a saint.	What is being a sinner?
The apostle Paul referred to himself as this.	Who is "chief of sinners"?
The Latin phrase Lutherans like to use to describe how one believer can be two persons at the same time.	What is *simul iustus et peccator*?
A Latin word that means "justified one" or "saint."	What is *iustus*?
The Lutheran answer to the question "Can the finite bear the infinite?"	What is "Yes!"?
This is what you are if you think you are not a sinner because you sometimes keep the Commandments.	What is "blissfully deluded"?

Multimedia Option

In *Chocolat* (2000; PG-13) we meet an excellent example of a sinner/saint in Comte Paul de Reynaud (Alfred Molina). As mayor of a little French town, Comte (Count) de Reynaud has spent the season of Lent exhorting his citizens to better moral living. Unfortunately, his efforts have been countered by the appearance of a newcomer, the enchanting Vianne Rocher (Juliette Binoche) and her newly opened *chocolaterie*. The scene opens with Comte de Reynaud giving the town's young priest (Hugh O'Conor) some pointers for his Easter sermon. When the Comte peeks out the window only to see his favorite parishioner enter the *chocolaterie*, he seeks the Lord's guidance. This leads to the Comte's "fall into sin" and, ultimately, to his redemption. (Some of the characters speak in low tones and with accents; you may want to turn on the English subtitles to make the dialogue easier to understand.)

Start the DVD at 1:44:31 (black screen, voice of the young priest uttering the words "Christ has risen"); stop the DVD at 1:53:30 (where Comte de Reynaud nods at Vianne and Vianne smiles back).

Questions to ask:
- What do you think about Comte de Reynaud's suggestion that the Easter sermon should be about resurrecting the "moral awareness" of the parishioners?
- Did Jesus tell the Comte to cut the head off of the nude statue made of chocolate?
- Is eating chocolate a sin? Is eating it the way Comte de Reynaud eats it a sin?
- How does the Comte's sin (and Vianne's forgiveness) lead to his redemption?
- What did you think of the young priest's Easter message (which, as the narrator admits, was not his best)?

Small Group Stuff

Direct participants into small groups to discuss the questions on page 22 in the *Workbook*. Tell the groups what time to return for Wrap-Up. Be ready to answer questions as needed.

Wrap-Up

Invite participants to bring their small group discussions to a close. In the large group, ask participants to share examples of their responses to the small group discussion questions. To wrap up, invite responses to the following questions:
- When you hear about a highly visible Christian leader who gets caught in a highly visible sin, what might be the right way to respond? (What does it say about us that we don't always respond this way?)
- In the end, the sinful self will be put to death once and for all, while the saintly self will live eternally. Is that good news or bad news? (Those who answer "bad news" because they will miss a particular sin are only proving the point that the sinful self is alive and well!)

As a follow-up to the theme of this session, invite participants to look for examples of temptation that they can discuss next time. Also encourage participants to read the related material in *The Lutheran Handbook II*.

Closing Litany and Prayer

Note: The group response is based on 1 Timothy 1:15.

> **Leader: Gracious God, your Son came not to call the righteous, but sinners, to repentance.**
> Group: This saying is true and worthy of acceptance: Christ Jesus came into the world to save sinners.
> **Leader: O Lord, we give you thanks for the life, death, and resurrection of your Son, Jesus Christ, through whom we have become saints, though we are yet sinners.**
> Group: This saying is true and worthy of acceptance: Christ Jesus came into the world to save sinners.
> **Leader: O God, make us sanctified sinners to be the bearers of your good news.**
> Group: This saying is true and worthy of acceptance: Christ Jesus came into the world to save sinners.
> **Leader: Remember us in your kingdom, O Lord, and teach us to pray . . .**
> All: *Our Father . . . [lead the group in your preferred form of the Lord's Prayer] . . . Amen.*

Objective

This fifth session makes clear that "justification by grace through faith apart from works" is not a license to sin, but a literal inspiration to serve the neighbor.

Materials needed

○ name tags
○ Table Talk cards for Session 5
○ songbooks
○ a Bible
○ *The Lutheran Handbook II*
○ *The Lutheran Course II Workbook*
○ pens or pencils
○ Course DVD
○ DVD player and screen
○ DVD of *Men in Black* (optional)
○ sheets of paper
○ colored pencils, crayons, and/or markers
○ tape

HOW TO IDENTIFY A "NEIGHBOR" AND WHAT THIS MEANS FOR LUTHERANS (If we're saved, can we do whatever we want?)

Overview

At this point, you wouldn't be the first person to ask, "If God makes me righteous by grace through faith, and if I'm a saint because of the cross of Christ, and if, as a saint, I'm still a sinner after all, then why not just go ahead and sin away?" Two thousand years ago, the Christians in Rome asked the apostle Paul the same question: "If God is gracious to sinners, should we continue in sin in order that grace may abound?" (Romans 6:1). You can sense the exasperation in Paul's response: *Is that really what you want? Don't you realize how sin harms you—not only you, but your neighbor even more so? What's wrong with you people?* Indeed, only the inner sinner in us would ask such a question.

On the other hand, as a new creation, your inner saint has no interest in continuing in sin (been there; done that). Instead, the "new you" wants to know, *Now that God has freely justified me by grace through faith, how can I best serve my neighbor?* Such a question makes no sense to your self-focused sinner. But to your self-giving saint, it makes all the sense in the world. This is why God created you after all: to take care of the earth and serve those who live in it. More on your proper vocation in Session 7—for now we'll concentrate on identifying the person who is the true beneficiary of your justification: namely, your neighbor.

The Lutheran Handbook II readings for this session:
pp. 72–74, 139–41, 153–54, 244–45, 289–90

Session 5

Table Talk

Participants will discuss these questions as they arrive:
- Is there such a thing as a stupid question?
- Have you ever watched *Mister Rogers' Neighborhood*? Did you enjoy it? (Come on, you can admit it.)
- Describe the best neighbors you've known.
- Is it ever a bad idea to be a "good Samaritan"?

Suggest that one person at each table pick up a Table Talk card at random, respond to the question, and pass the card to the person to the right, who will also answer the question and pass the card on. When that card has gone around the table, someone else can pick up another card and repeat the process until time is up.

Large Group Stuff

Opening

Welcome participants and review the last session. Ask for examples of temptation that participants have noted since the previous session. Next, invite responses to the Table Talk items for this session.

Give a brief introduction to the session. For example: "Now that we have covered the cross of Christ and the justification of sinners by grace through faith apart from works, you might be wondering, *So what's left?* Why, your neighbor, of course! There are people out there who could use your help and support. If you want to love your neighbor as yourself, you have to (a) get over yourself and (b) get over to where you can do your neighbor some good. Who is your neighbor? That's what we're about to find out."

Read or have a participant read the Overview on page 24 of the *Workbook*.

Session preparation
- ○ Read the session material in this *Leader Book*, the *Workbook*, and the *Handbook*.
- ○ Preview the entire DVD presentation.
- ○ Set up DVD player and screen.
- ○ Cue DVD.
- ○ Set up refreshments.

Table Talk preparation
- ○ Make copies of the Table Talk cards on page 93.
- ○ Cut on the dotted lines.
- ○ Place a set of four cards on each table.

Hymn suggestions

The earthly aim of justification by grace through faith is to free you up for service to the neighbor. The following songs have this aim in mind.
- *ELW* 546
- *ELW* 650
- *ELW* 659
- *ELW* 708
- *ELW* 716

Christian freedom doesn't mean doing whatever we want, without thinking about our neighbors.

Invite a participant to read the key scripture text for this session: "What then are we to say? Should we continue in sin in order that grace may abound?" (Romans 6:1). This question is rhetorical; that is, the question is asked with the right answer already in mind. And the answer is: No way! Grace does not lead to self-indulgence. Instead, Lutherans are confident that the word of the cross will get you beyond yourself and get you thinking about your neighbor—not because you have to, but because you *want* to!

Introduce the opening prayer (*ELW*, p. 42) with the following exchange:

Leader: The Lord be with you.
 Group: And also with you.
Leader: Let us pray. . . .

O Lord God, your mercy delights us, and the world longs for your loving care. Hear the cries of everyone in need, and turn our hearts to love our neighbors with the love of your Son, Jesus Christ, our Savior and Lord. Amen.

Video

Introduce the video: For this session on the freedom of a Christian, our narrator travels to Wartburg College in Waverly, Iowa, to speak with Peter T. Nash, visiting professor of religion and special assistant to the president for global communities; and Wartburg College students.

Play the Session 5 DVD presentation in its entirety. After the presentation, ask for any initial reactions. (Receive all responses.) Which person in the video was most intriguing? Why?

Large Group Activity

❶ In this activity group members will exercise their artistic talents by making a comic book version of Jesus' parable of the good Samaritan (Luke 10:25–37). Here's how:
- Explain to participants that they will create a panel cartoon for a parable told by Jesus.
- Distribute the sheets of paper, pens or pencils, and colored pencils, crayons, and/or markers.
- Invite someone to read Luke 10:25–37 aloud; encourage the rest to listen closely.
- Assign individuals (or pairs) to illustrate any or all of the following scenes. You can divide the scenes in any way that suits your group.

Panel What to Draw
1. A lawyer stands to test Jesus, asking: "What must I do to inherit eternal life?"
2. Jesus asks the lawyer: "What is written in the law?"
3. The lawyer says: "Love your neighbor as yourself."
4. Jesus says: "You have given the right answer; do this, and you will live."
5. The lawyer, wanting to justify himself, asks: "And who is my neighbor?"
6. Jesus says: "Have I got a story for you!"
7. A man traveled down the road from Jerusalem to Jericho one day.
8. Suddenly robbers fell upon the man; they beat him, stripped him, and left him for dead.
9. A priest traveling the road saw the man but passed by on the other side.
10. A Levite traveling the road saw the man but passed by on the other side.
11. A man from Samaria came by and, seeing the victim, was moved with pity.
12. The Samaritan wrapped the man's wounds and treated them with oil and wine.
13. The Samaritan put the beat-up man on his own horse.
14. The Samaritan brought the man to an inn.
15. The Samaritan gave the innkeeper money to take care of the beat-up man.
16. The Samaritan told the innkeeper that he would return and pay any additional costs.
17. Jesus asks: "Which of the three was a neighbor to the man who fell among robbers?"
18. The lawyer says: "The one who showed him mercy."
19. Jesus says: "Go and do likewise!"

- After all panels have been drawn, arrange them on a wall or board (fastening with tape, tacks, or magnets) in storyboard form.
- Review the entire passage, panel by panel. Ask artists to explain their contributions.
- Ask some follow-up questions, including:
  - Does it help to know that in tribal society, it would have been silly to think that the word *neighbor* could include someone from another nation or race?
  - Does it help to know that it may have been against the law for the priest and Levite to touch the man, since touching a dead body would have made them "impure" and, therefore, unable to perform their religious duties (see Numbers 19:11)?
  - Does it help to know the identity of the parable's original hearer, the lawyer who wanted "to justify himself"?

❷ Invite volunteers to read and discuss the six tips under "How to Identify a 'Neighbor' and What This Means for Lutherans" in *The Lutheran Handbook II* (pp. 153–54). Next, ask participants to name some less obvious "neighbors" in the spirit of the good Samaritan. These might include a man who is homeless, an immigrant, the girl working the drive-up window at the local fast-food joint, and so forth. Then challenge participants to name someone who is *not* a neighbor.

Multimedia Option

The movie *Men in Black* (1997; PG-13) has an interesting answer to the question "Who is my neighbor?" Like most law-enforcement agents, it is the duty of the Men in Black to protect and serve. In this far-out film, MIB agents Kay (Tommy Lee Jones) and Jay (Will Smith) are sworn to protect and serve the nation's alien population—as in outer-space alien population. (You see, unbeknownst to average citizens, there are space aliens disguised as humans living in our midst.) In this brief scene, agent-in-training Jay finds out the hard way that he is called to serve the neighbor—no matter what planet she's from. (Participants will surely note the pre-9/11 Twin Towers in prominent display in the backdrop of this scene.)

Start the DVD at 0:43:17 (as Agent Kay approaches the station wagon); stop the DVD at 0:45:28 (just after Agent Kay asks, "Did anything about that seem unusual to you?"). Another scene of interest comes at the beginning of the movie and features Agent Kay's neighborly treatment of earthly "illegal aliens" being smuggled over the border. (Start the DVD at 0:03:04; stop the DVD at 0:08:56.)

Questions to ask:
- With this scene in mind, is there anybody who is *not* your neighbor?
- With this scene in mind, is there anything you should *not* do to help your neighbor?

Small Group Stuff

Direct participants into small groups to discuss the questions on page 26 in the *Workbook*. Tell the groups what time to return for Wrap-Up. Be ready to answer questions as needed.

Anyone in need is your neighbor.

Wrap-Up

Invite participants to bring their small group discussions to a close. In the large group ask them to share examples of their responses to the small group discussion questions. To wrap-up, invite responses to the following questions:
- Since serving your neighbor won't earn you salvation, list some of the other reasons you would want to serve your neighbor.
- What are some of the factors that prevent you from loving your neighbor as yourself?

As a follow-up to the theme of this session, invite participants to look for examples of various freedoms and of service to neighbors. Also encourage participants to read the related material in *The Lutheran Handbook II*.

Closing Litany and Prayer (based on Philippians 2:5–12)

Leader: The Lord be with you.

Group: And also with you.

Leader: Let us pray. Lord, give to us the same mind that was in Christ Jesus, who did not take advantage of his divinity, but who instead emptied himself, becoming human, that he might serve humanity; and humbled himself unto death—even death on a cross. Therefore, O God, you have exalted your Son, giving him the name that is above every name,

Group: So that at the name of Jesus, every knee will bend and every tongue will confess that Jesus Christ is Lord.

Leader: Therefore, O God, as we work out with fear and trembling the salvation you have already given us, help us to remember that you are at work in us, enabling us to will and to work according to your good pleasure.

Group: So that at the name of Jesus, every knee will bend and every tongue will confess that Jesus Christ is Lord.

Leader: Remember us in your kingdom, O Lord, and teach us to pray . . .

All: *Our Father . . . [lead the group in your preferred form of the Lord's Prayer] . . . Amen.*

HOW TO TELL THE DIFFERENCE BETWEEN THE KINGDOM ON THE LEFT AND THE KINGDOM ON THE RIGHT (Should Christians be involved in the world?)

Session 6

Objective
This session introduces participants to Luther's idea that God reigns over humans under two kingdoms: a left-hand, or earthly, kingdom and a right-hand, or heavenly, kingdom.

Materials needed
- name tags
- Table Talk cards for Session 6
- songbooks
- a Bible
- *The Lutheran Handbook II*
- *The Lutheran Course II Workbook*
- pens or pencils
- Course DVD
- DVD player and screen
- A version of the board game Monopoly® (Hasbro Inc.)
- DVD of *Bruce Almighty* (optional)

Overview

So far, we've seen that Lutherans use "two-handed thinking" to explain things such as bound will and free will, saints and sinners, and freedom and servanthood. Lutherans also use this way of thinking to describe God's two-handed approach in dealing with humans. On the one hand, the New Testament has much to say about the "kingdom come"—the kingdom of heaven, in which Jesus rules at God's *right hand*. On the other hand, God is involved with running things here on earth, too. God's rule over the earth is what Lutherans have called the kingdom on God's *left hand*.

Here's how God's two-handed reign works. Through the kingdom on the *left hand*, God provides governments and institutions (including family and church!) to keep law and order. All people, sinners that we are, need to be compelled to obey the law—or else! Can you imagine this world without rules, or without consequences for breaking those rules? Neither can God. That's why, this side of heaven, God still needs to rule through institutions that wield "the sword"—that is, through law and through consequences for breaking the law.

The Lutheran Handbook II readings for this session:
pp. 120–21, 168–69, 174–77, 262–64, 285–88

Session preparation
○ Read the session material in this *Leader Book*, the *Workbook*, and the *Handbook*.
○ Preview the entire DVD presentation.
○ Set up DVD player and screen.
○ Cue DVD.
○ Set up refreshments.

Table Talk preparation
○ Make copies of the Table Talk cards on page 94.
○ Cut on the dotted lines.
○ Place a set of four cards on each table.

Because Christians are not only sinners, but saints as well, God also rules via the kingdom on the *right hand*. In this right-hand kingdom, God does not rule by institutions enforcing laws. Instead, God rules by transforming hearts and lives with the Spirit of Jesus Christ. Through the gospel, God moves saints to do good works, not because they *have to* by law, but because they *want to*, simply out of love for the neighbor.

Table Talk

Participants will discuss these questions as they arrive:
- Do you know anyone who is ambidextrous (equally capable from the left or right side)?
- Are you "left-brained" (more logical and detail oriented) or "right-brained" (more creative and big-picture oriented)?
- Summarize a fairy tale or movie that involves a king and/or a queen.
- What ruler or leader are you most like? (This can be a fictional character, historical figure, or present-day person.)

Suggest that one person at each table pick up a Table Talk card at random, respond to the question, and pass the card to the person to the right, who will also answer the question and pass the card on. When that card has gone around the table, someone else can pick up another card and repeat the process until time is up.

Large Group Stuff

Opening

Welcome participants and review the last session. Ask for examples of freedoms and of service to neighbors that participants have noted since the previous session. Next, invite responses to the Table Talk items for this session.

Give a brief introduction to the session. For example: "What is God up to in the world? The Lutheran idea about God reigning with both the left hand and the right hand is one way to respond to this question."

Session 6

Read or have a participant read the Overview on page 28 of the *Workbook*.

Invite a participant to read the key scripture text for this session: "As you have sent me into the world, so I have sent them into the world" (John 17:18). The arrival of Jesus in the world is accompanied by the announcement "The kingdom of heaven has come near" (Matthew 3:2; Mark 1:15). As followers of Jesus, we are, in a way, dual citizens—citizens of heaven and of earth. That said, Christ does not call us to escape the earthly kingdom. Instead, we are sent into the earthly realm as ambassadors of the heavenly realm.

Introduce the opening prayer with the following exchange:

> **Leader: The Lord be with you.**
> Group: And also with you.
> **Leader: Let us pray. . . .**

Almighty and heavenly God, creator of the world, we give you thanks and praise for all you have made. We give you thanks for the beauty of the earth and for the wonder of nature. We give you thanks that you have created us in your image, that we might be gathered in community with you and with one another. Make us, O Lord, to reflect your goodness in the world; through Jesus Christ, your Son, our Lord. Amen.

Hymn suggestions
These hymns give praise to God, who rules the kingdom on the left and the kingdom on the right.
- *ELW* 632
- *ELW* 654
- *ELW* 834
- *ELW* 836
- *ELW* 839
- *ELW* 855
- *ELW* 856

God's Kingdom on the Left *God's Kingdom on the Right*

Leader Book 69

Video

Introduce the video: For this session on the kingdom on the left and the kingdom on the right, our narrator travels to New York City to speak with Stephen P. Bouman, bishop, Metropolitan New York Synod; and members of St. Luke's Lutheran Church, near Times Square. (The conversation with Bishop Bouman was filmed at the offices of Lutheran Disaster Response of New York.)

Play the Session 6 DVD presentation in its entirety. After the presentation, ask for any initial reactions. (Receive all responses.) Which person in the video was most intriguing? Why?

Large Group Activity

❶ Note: To save time, you may want to set up the board game in advance. You may even want to distribute some or all of the property deeds in advance.

The idea of God's two kingdoms underlies many discussions that Christians have regarding ethical behavior. For instance, in Luther's day, people were concerned about whether or not Christian behavior was compatible with holding civil office, serving in the military, or charging interest on loans. By distinguishing between God's two kingdoms, Lutherans have been able to say, *yes*, Christians can and should serve the world by participating in worldly institutions. In Luther's view, even the executioner could serve as a Christian, provided he carried out his duties faithfully and with honor!

To demonstrate how tough it is for us to conduct ourselves as heavenly citizens in the earthly kingdom, play Monopoly® (Hasbro Inc.).
- Split the large group into three to six teams of at least two players each.

- Split each team into those who are grace oriented and those who are not. Explain to those who are to be grace oriented that the goal is not to win, but to be gracious. Explain to those who are not to be grace oriented that the goal is to win at all costs. Explain that team members may have to make some compromises for the game to progress.
- Begin playing the game. Watch the sparks fly.
- After playing for several minutes, ask some follow-up questions, such as:
  - Are property acquisition and Christianity compatible?
  - How do terms such as *faithful, honorable, trustworthy*, and *moderate* apply to questions about how Christians should conduct themselves in the world?
  - What would Jesus do?

We are not called to separate ourselves from the world. God is at work in the world, and we are called to be at work there, too.

❷ Invite volunteers to take turns reading portions of "How to Tell the Difference between the Kingdom on the Left and the Kingdom on the Right," beginning on page 174 of *The Lutheran Handbook II*. Next, invite the group to think of examples of situations that reflect the tension between the two kingdoms. Here are just a few possibilities:
- A Christian police officer clocks you going 65 mph in a 55 mph (100 km/h in an 80 km/h) zone.
- A Christian parent tries to determine the best way to discipline a child who continues to repeat the same bad behavior.
- A Christian professor must decide whether or not to report a student for plagiarism.
- A Christian defense attorney must defend a client who has privately admitted to being guilty of the crime.
- A Christian judge must rule in a murder case in which the defendant has expressed great remorse, but the victim's family wants the maximum penalty.
- A Christian leader is considering taking military action that will cost the lives of hundreds if not thousands of soldiers.

Facilitate discussion on the follow-up questions. How should Christians conduct themselves in positions of worldly authority? What are the contingencies? Is it enough to ask, "What would Jesus do?"

Multimedia Option

At the beginning of the movie *Bruce Almighty* (2003; PG-13), things are not going well for Bruce Nolan (Jim Carrey). Bruce gets angry and blames God for all that is wrong with his life. Bruce even goes so far as to throw his prayer beads into Lake Erie. God (played by Morgan Freeman) decides that enough is enough. God summons Bruce for a face-to-face meeting. In this scene, God confronts Bruce with his self-centered complaining. To teach Bruce a lesson about how tough it is to reign over everything, the Almighty decides to let Bruce try being God for a while.

Start the DVD at 0:25:18 (where Bruce arrives at the warehouse for his meeting with God); stop the DVD at 0:41:00 (where God walks off and "Bruce Almighty" is left to walk on water by himself). If 15 minutes is too long for your meeting time, you may stop the DVD at 0:35:49 (just after Bruce parts the waters in his bowl of soup).

Questions to ask:
- What do you think would be the hardest part of doing God's job? (A bit later in the movie, Bruce is awakened by millions of voices in his head. Bruce realizes that these are the prayers of millions of people around the world. Bruce, as God, must figure out a way to track the prayers and then respond to each one.)
- In his instructions to Bruce, God warns Bruce that he can't "mess with free will." Although Lutherans hold there is no free will in terms of salvation, there is free will in "things below"—that is, here on earth. What would it say about God if humans had no free will at all—if every human action was programmed in advance?

Small Group Stuff

Direct participants into small groups to discuss the questions on page 30 in the *Workbook*. Tell the groups what time to return for Wrap-Up. Be ready to answer questions as needed.

Wrap-Up

Invite participants to bring their small group discussions to a close. In the large group, ask participants to share examples of their responses to the small group discussion questions. To wrap up, invite responses to the following questions:
- Now that you've thought about it, would you really want to have the job of creator and sustainer of the universe? Or is being a plain old creature more appealing all of a sudden?

- How does the notion of God's two kingdoms fit with the question "Why do bad things happen to good people?"

As a follow-up to the theme of this session, invite participants to look for ways they bring their faith into their daily lives. Also encourage participants to read the related material in *The Lutheran Handbook II*.

Closing Litany and Prayer

Leader: The Lord be with you.
Group: And also with you.
Leader: Let us pray. God, our creator and sustainer of the universe, you rule heaven and earth.
Group: Your kingdom come. Your will be done, on earth as in heaven.
Leader: You rule heaven by transforming hearts and lives with the Spirit of Jesus Christ. Transform us and guide us to carry out your will.
Group: Your kingdom come. Your will be done, on earth as in heaven.
Leader: You rule the earth by providing governments and institutions to keep law and order. Give wisdom to leaders around the world, and guide them to carry out your will.
Group: Your kingdom come. Your will be done, on earth as in heaven.
Leader: You prepare a place for us in heaven, and you send us into the world, too. By your grace, equip us to serve you while serving our neighbors.
Group: Your kingdom come. Your will be done, on earth as in heaven.
Leader: Remember us in your kingdom, O Lord, and teach us to pray . . .
All: *Our Father . . . [lead the group in your preferred form of the Lord's Prayer] . . . Amen.*

HOW TO TELL THE DIFFERENCE BETWEEN A "VOCATION" AND A "VACATION" (Can we make a difference in this world?)

Session 7

Objective
This final session illustrates how "vocation" is more than "just a job" (from which you need a vacation)—it is everything God calls people to do to serve the neighbor and all that God has made.

Overview
• • • • •

If all the talk about the cross and sin and captivity makes you suspect that Lutheran theology is designed to keep people down, you are right, in a way. Luther *did* want to keep people down; that is, he wanted to keep them down to earth—down to the good earth God created in the beginning! Lutheran Christians believe there is something to that old complaint about people who are too religious: "They've become so heavenly minded that they're no earthly good." The gospel of Jesus, Luther says, is not about humans working their way *up* to heaven; instead, it is all about God coming *down* to earth, becoming fully human. And God does this so that humans can become fully human as well.

As a young monk, Luther believed that being saved and getting into heaven meant putting aside the cares of the world. Through the gospel, however, Luther came to realize that caring for the world was humanity's true and original vocation. As radical as this idea was in his day, Luther's view of vocation went even further. Many people at the time believed priests, monks, and nuns lived a "spiritual life" that was a sort of permanent vacation from "nonspiritual" vocations such as working a job, being a spouse, and raising a child. Luther, meanwhile, came to understand that through the gospel, the most mundane tasks can be spiritual callings.

Materials needed
- name tags
- Table Talk cards for Session 7
- songbooks
- a Bible
- *The Lutheran Handbook II*
- *The Lutheran Course II Workbook*
- pens or pencils
- Course DVD
- DVD player and screen
- DVD of *National Lampoon's Vacation* (optional)
- copies of the Course Evaluation Form on page 96 in this *Leader Book*

Session preparation
○ Read the session material in this *Leader Book*, the *Workbook*, and the *Handbook*.
○ Preview the entire DVD presentation.
○ Set up DVD player and screen.
○ Cue DVD.
○ Set up refreshments.

Table Talk preparation
○ Make copies of the Table Talk cards on page 95.
○ Cut on the dotted lines.
○ Place a set of four cards on each table.

The Lutheran Handbook II readings for this session:
pp. 155–57, 158–60, 164–67, 193–95, 258–61

Table Talk

Participants will discuss these questions as they arrive:
- Name an exotic vacation destination.
- Give an example of a tough job (but someone's gotta do it).
- Give an example of a spiritual calling.
- Define *vocation* (and while you're at it, define *vacation*).

Suggest that one person at each table pick up a Table Talk card at random, respond to the question, and pass the card to the person to the right, who will also answer the question and pass the card on. When that card has gone around the table, someone else can pick up another card and repeat the process until time is up.

Large Group Stuff

Opening

Welcome participants. Ask for examples of faith in daily life that participants have noted since the previous session. Next, invite responses to the Table Talk items for this session.

Give a brief introduction to the session. For example: "In this session, we'll look at the Lutheran idea of *vocation*. The word *vocation* is based on the Latin word *vocare*, 'to call.' We'll consider what it means to have a divine call—if not many divine calls—in life."

Session 7

Read or have a participant read the Overview on page 32 of the *Workbook*.

Invite a participant to read the key scripture text for this session: "For we are what he has made us, created in Christ Jesus for good works, which God prepared beforehand to be our way of life" (Ephesians 2:10). Explain how this passage comes right on the tail of the key scripture from Session 3: "For by grace you have been saved through faith, and this is not your own doing; it is the gift of God—not the result of works, so that no one may boast" (Ephesians 2:8-9). Taken together, these verses spell out the relationship between justification and vocation. That is, through the cross of Christ, God not only frees us *from* sin, God also frees us *for* service to neighbor.

Introduce the opening prayer with the following exchange:

    Leader: The Lord be with you.
     Group: And also with you.
    Leader: Let us pray. . . .

God of all creation: In the beginning, you created us in your image. You created us to be caretakers of your world and of those who live in it. Yet we have failed in this calling. Forgive us, Lord, and re-create us for faithful service in your name; through Jesus Christ, your Son, our Lord. Amen.

Hymn suggestions
These hymns testify to God's call in all that we do as stewards of God's creation and caretakers of one another.
- *ELW 574*
- *ELW 679*
- *ELW 685*
- *ELW 712*
- *ELW 729*
- *ELW 818*

A Vacation   *A Vocation*

Leader Book 77

Video

Introduce the video: For this session on vocation, our narrator travels to Minnesota to speak with Mary Jane Haemig, associate professor of church history and director of the Thrivent Reformation Research Program, Luther Seminary, St. Paul; and members of Spirit Garage, Minneapolis.

Play the Session 7 DVD presentation in its entirety. After the presentation, ask for any initial reactions. (Receive all responses.) Which person in the video was most intriguing? Why?

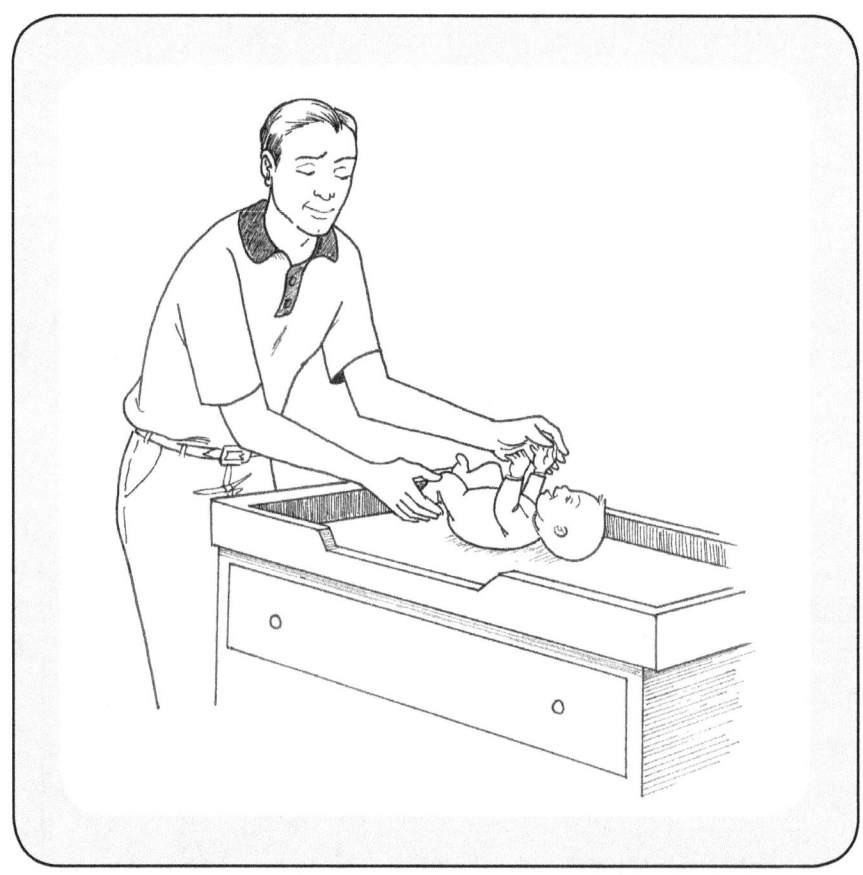

Luther's understanding of marriage as a vocation led him to say that even changing a baby's diapers was part of carrying out God's will.

Session 7

Large Group Activity

❶ In Luther's day, there were two levels of workers: those who were part of the "spiritual estate" (bishops, priests, nuns, and so forth) and just about everybody else. Mundane work was seen as important, but not very spiritual. (Note: The word *mundane* is based on the Latin word *mundus*, translated "world.") The large group activity for this session is designed to expose our two-tiered thinking regarding our work in the world.

Direct participants to the large group activity on page 33 of the *Workbook*. Invite them to rank the various activities listed there from 1 to 10, with 1 being the most spiritual and 10 being the least spiritual. Clarify any items (for instance, a "vow of chastity" refers to the celibacy pledge that Roman Catholic priests make). After you've given participants sufficient time to complete the exercise, invite them to share the top three items on their list. Except for those who are clued into the gist of this session, most participants will put things such as going to church, reading the Bible, and praying at the top of their lists. Parents might also put raising children at the top of their lists. Invite participants to offer other activities they consider to be spiritual and not-so-spiritual. Ask participants to offer reasons for their rankings. These reasons will expose their understanding of the word *spiritual*.

Offer the following explanation: "As a monk, Martin Luther had this insight: even the most religious deed that is done in the hope that it will earn favor with God is not really a spiritual activity. Instead, Luther saw such activity as worldly, since the focus was on human rather than divine work. On the other hand, Luther came to understand that God's original intention for humans was for them to take care of the earth and of each other. Properly understood, such work—no matter how earthly—was truly spiritual work, since through such work, God created and continues to create the world. As Luther himself put it: 'God's people please God even in the least and most trifling matters. For [God] will be working all things through you; [God] will milk the cow through you and perform the most servile duties through you' (*Luther's Works* 6:10)."

Leader Book 79

❷ If there is time, read "How to Tell the Difference between a 'Vocation' and a 'Vacation,'" beginning on page 164 of *The Lutheran Handbook II*. Ask participants to respond to these items with their comments or questions. The first three items are lighthearted and may generate discussion about what constitutes a good vacation. The last three items get at some of the real issues of our earthly vocations: Are they appreciated? Are they challenging? Are they fulfilling? Luther saw that our vocations are, in one sense, burdens we bear for the benefit of others. In this sense, human vocation takes on the dimension of the cross of Christ. For those who are faltering under the weight of their vocation(s), Christ offers these words: "Come to me, all you that are weary and are carrying heavy burdens, and I will give you rest. Take my yoke upon you, and learn from me. . . . For my yoke is easy, and my burden is light" (Matthew 11:28-30).

Multimedia Option

National Lampoon's Vacation (1983; R) is probably not the kind of movie you will want to show in polite and/or mixed company. That said, you can dig out a couple of clips in the film that get at both of the subjects of this session: vacation *and* vocation. One such clip involves the scene in the motel restaurant, where Clark Griswold (Chevy Chase) meets "the girl in the Ferrari" (Christy Brinkley). In this scene, Clark has snuck away from his family's motel room to relax over a drink. At the bar, Clark encounters the mysterious woman who's been flirting with him on the road. They begin a conversation—a conversation in which Clark explains that he's really *not* an average family man with an average job taking an average vacation with his average family, but that he's actually a former CIA man on a covert mission—the average family/job thing is just a cover.

Start the DVD at 1:09:41 (with Clark in the bar); stop the DVD at 1:13:04 (as Clark and the woman leave the bar). It is up to your discretion to choose to show the next scene, the infamous "pool scene" (which goes through 1:16:30). In this scene, Clark's true vocation of an average family man is "exposed." (Caution: The pool scene contains people in their underwear and implied nudity, as well as one profanity and one violation of the commandment that forbids taking the Lord's name in vain.)

Questions to ask (based only on the scene in the bar):
- Why does Clark lie about his real job?
- What is the relationship between vocation and the commandment that forbids adultery?
- What is it that makes living a quiet life of humble service to others seem so unattractive?

Small Group Stuff

Direct participants into small groups to discuss the questions on page 34 in the *Workbook*. Tell the groups what time to return for Wrap-Up. Be ready to answer questions as needed.

Wrap-Up

Invite participants to bring their small group discussions to a close. In the large group ask participants to share examples of their responses to the small group discussion questions. To wrap-up, invite responses to the following questions:
- What are the challenges of balancing family life, work life, civic life, and church life? In our culture, which vocational "realm" (family, work, civic, church) gets the most emphasis or attention?
- Which of your present roles or duties is most burdensome? Viewed through the lens of faith, is it possible to transform this "tough job" into a burden that is borne for the sake of the neighbor?
- How can the church and its leaders help you to discern and appreciate your various vocations?

Close your time together by inviting general feedback regarding the seven sessions overall. Thank participants for their involvement in this course. Encourage them to continue studying the Bible and God's activity in the world. Also encourage them to consider the question "Now that I don't have to do anything to be saved, what am I going to do?"

Distribute copies of the Course Evaluation Form. Ask participants to fill out and return the form before they leave today.

Closing Litany and Prayer

Leader: **The Lord be with you.**
Group: And also with you.
Leader: **Let us pray. Gracious God, you have made us to be your hands and your feet in the world.**
Group: You created us in your image; you blessed us to be a blessing.
Leader: **Yet we have failed to love our neighbors as ourselves.**
Group: You created us in your image; you blessed us to be a blessing.
Leader: **In baptism you call us into a new life; forgiving our sin, you renew us in love and strengthen us for service.**
Group: You created us in your image; you blessed us to be a blessing.
Leader: **We thank you for our time together and for the encouragement we have received through your Holy Word. Now send us forth in your name.**
Group: You created us in your image; you blessed us to be a blessing.
Leader: **Remember us in your kingdom, O Lord, and teach us to pray . . .**
All: *Our Father . . . [lead the group in your preferred form of the Lord's Prayer] . . . Amen.*

COURSE OVERVIEW

Session 1: How to Tell the Difference between Theology of the Cross and Theology of Glory (How does God work?)
Theme: The cross is key to salvation and the way God works.
Congregational visit: Trinity Evangelical Lutheran Church, Lansdale, PA
Featuring a conversation with Timothy J. Wengert, Ministerium of Pennsylvania Professor, Reformation History, The Lutheran Theological Seminary at Philadelphia, Philadelphia, PA

Session 2: How to Tell If Your Will Is in Bondage to Sin and What to Do about It (Why do we do things we know we shouldn't do?)
Theme: We need God's grace because we are bound to sin.
Congregational visit: Coon Valley Lutheran Church, Coon Valley, WI
Featuring a conversation with April Ulring Larson, Bishop, LaCrosse Area Synod, LaCrosse, WI

Session 3: How to Receive God's Grace Daily (How are we saved?)
Theme: God gives us grace, forgiveness, and salvation through the cross.
Congregational visit: Lutheran Church of the Redeemer, Atlanta, GA
Featuring a conversation with Lawrence J. Clark, Executive Director, Lutheran Theological Center in Atlanta, Atlanta, GA

Session 4: How to Tell the Difference between a Sinner and a Saint (If we're saved, why do we still sin?)
Theme: God saves us even though we are sinners.
Congregational visit: Shepherd of the Hills Lutheran Church, Berkeley, CA
Featuring a conversation with Martha E. Stortz, Professor of Historical Theology and Ethics, and Jane E. Strohl, Associate Professor of Church History and Reformation History, Pacific Lutheran Theological Seminary, Berkeley, CA

Session 5: How to Identify a "Neighbor" and What This Means for Lutherans (If we're saved, can we do whatever we want?)
Theme: Christ frees us from the law so that we are free to serve others.
Congregational visit: Wartburg College students, Waverly, IA
Featuring a conversation with Peter T. Nash, Visiting Professor of Religion and Special Assistant to the President for Global Communities, Wartburg College, Waverly, IA

Session 6: How to Tell the Difference between the Kingdom on the Left and the Kingdom on the Right (Should Christians be involved in the world?)
Theme: God is at work in the world, and we are called to be at work there, too.
Congregational visit: St. Luke's Lutheran Church, New York City, NY
Featuring a conversation with Stephen P. Bouman, Bishop, Metropolitan New York Synod, New York City, NY (filmed at Lutheran Disaster Response of New York)

Session 7: How to Tell the Difference between a "Vocation" and a "Vacation" (Can we make a difference in this world?)
Theme: Any job, career, or role is holy when it's done as part of the baptismal call from God to serve others.
Congregational visit: Spirit Garage, Minneapolis, MN
Featuring a conversation with Mary Jane Haemig, Director, Thrivent Reformation Research Program, Associate Professor of Church History, Luther Seminary, St. Paul, MN

SMALL GROUP LEADER'S GUIDE

A small group that is functioning properly is like a well-oiled machine. It hums along in confidence, completing its job smoothly. But a small group that is not functioning well is more like a machine that is plunking along in spurts and fits, sometimes stopping, and only once in a while achieving the goal for which it was designed. And just like a good mechanic who makes sure a machine is purring like a kitten, a capable small group leader is someone who carefully facilitates the flow of ideas and insights generated by the group so that they move along with ease and enthusiasm.

So what makes some small groups fall off track while others run without a glitch? Well, small groups that are in trouble usually have a few things in common. Perhaps there is a dominant member who consumes most of the time and air in the room, or the discussion often veers off the topic, or someone shares too much personal information. Bad group experiences seem to stick in our minds for a long time and actually overshadow the good that could come out of small groups. So we definitely want to avoid these pitfalls.

What about small groups that hum along in health? What makes experiences in these groups so comfortable and refreshing? In small groups that hum along, group members tend to share "air time" so that everyone has an opportunity to share appropriately and without interruption. Instead of taking detours into unrelated areas, the group works together to keep the discussion on track. Group members respect personal boundaries and don't share or intrude beyond the level of comfort or appropriateness. When a small group is functioning well, it generally is following a set of principles or guidelines, similar to these, to help it purr along:

- We agree to make these sessions a priority in our lives and to attend faithfully.
- We agree to pray for one another.
- We agree to listen to one another.
- We agree to share from our own insights and experience—to speak for "self"—and to avoid the temptation to speak for others or to advise or direct other members in our group.
- We agree to share freely with one another our questions, discoveries, struggles, and feelings about topics raised in *The Lutheran Course II*.

The Lutheran Course II Leader Book, copyright © 2007 Augsburg Fortress.
May be reproduced for local use.

- We agree to keep personal things spoken in our times together within the circle of our group, maintaining an atmosphere of confidentiality, openness, and trust.

You'll find these exact guidelines in the Small Group Covenant for this course. (See page 7 in the *Workbook*.)

Your Responsibilities as a Small Group Leader

Guiding the Small Group Experience
As the small group leader, you will guide the small group experience. The Small Group Covenant sets the stage for you by giving clear expectations for each session. In the first session, discuss the Small Group Covenant and go over it so everyone has the same working definition of each item. Be sure to highlight regular participation and the importance of honoring confidentiality.

Introduce the concept of speaking for "self," and let group members know exactly what that means. Help them understand that speaking for "self" means sharing personal perspectives, thoughts, feelings, and ideas that are best expressed using "I" statements, such as, "I really like . . ." or "I have struggled with . . .". Speaking for self does not include speaking for a spouse or anyone else in the group.

Discussing topics such as sin, grace, service, and vocation occasionally brings deep feelings of guilt, unworthiness, regret, and uncertainty to the surface. If someone shares something with the group or with you that needs further attention, share your concerns with that person privately and, if there is interest, suggest a conversation with the pastor.

Creating a Comfortable Small Group Environment
As the small group leader, you will be facilitating the discussions each time you meet. In this role, you are not asked to impart any theological doctrine, central truth, or special knowledge. You are simply responsible to help the group begin its conversation, help the conversation continue, and make sure everyone has a chance to speak. While you will want to give each person an opportunity to take part in the conversation, some people are naturally more expressive while others tend to be quiet and retiring. Part of creating a safe and inviting environment for your small group is to give everyone the right to pass if they don't feel like speaking at the moment.

In addition to priming and supporting the small group discussion, you are also called upon to help all group members respect one another and their differing opinions, beliefs, and perspectives. Clearly, when we are talking about faith, not everyone in your small group will be in the same place in his or her thinking. Even for lifelong Lutherans, some of the ideas in *The Lutheran Handbook II* and *The Lutheran Course II* may seem new and foreign. And this will more than likely generate some energized conversation. Therefore, your

The Lutheran Course II Leader Book, copyright © 2007 Augsburg Fortress.
May be reproduced for local use.

role as the small group leader is to allow group members to explore these new ideas in a respectful environment that supports curiosity and discovery.

Helping Group Members Connect
The small group experience can be very powerful as group members connect and glean from each other's experiences. To help facilitate this connection, you'll want to spend some time in each session just chatting so that group members get to know one another. This will make it easier for people to talk openly about matters of faith later in the session. So make sure that you dedicate some time in each session to simply sharing joys and sorrows that have occurred since the last meeting, and then include the most significant of these joys and sorrows in a group prayer, perhaps immediately or just before the small group discussion concludes. And don't feel that you, as leader, must always be in charge of these prayers. You can certainly invite others to take turns at different meetings, or ask everyone to offer portions of the prayer around the circle.

Exploring Small Group Stuff
The Small Group Stuff section in the *Workbook* provides tools to start and continue conversations. It's important to read over all of the questions for each session so you can decide how you would like to use them during your small group gathering. Although there will be time during Wrap-Up to share feedback and responses with the larger group, there is no pressure to use every question in the sessions. If one or two items launch enough conversation for the entire time you are together, then you have really accomplished your primary goal of facilitating the group's conversation. To loosely apply Mark 2:27, the *Workbook* was made for you, not you for the *Workbook*.

Having Fun
Have fun and enjoy getting to know everyone in your group! As the group grows more comfortable and learns the routine and the safe ground rules established in the Small Group Covenant, it will depend on you less and less. Then you'll be able to settle in and enjoy the fruits of a well-functioning group.

Future Options
At the end of the last session of the course, your small group might consider future options. Some groups will choose to simply disband as the course comes to an end. Other small groups will want to continue meeting even after the course ends. Rest assured that your commitment as small group leader is only for the sessions of this course. There are no hidden expectations. If the group decides to continue meeting, you may continue in a leadership role, or group members may elect a different small group leader, or they may rotate group leadership among themselves. The best thing to do is to wait and see what happens.

So for now, thank you for being a small group leader for *The Lutheran Course II*!

The Lutheran Course II Leader Book, copyright © 2007 Augsburg Fortress.
May be reproduced for local use.

Session 1

TABLE TALK

Think of words or terms that contain the word *cross* (for instance, *cross section* or *crossed fingers*). How many can you name?

TABLE TALK

Think of words or terms that contain the word *cross* (for instance, *cross section* or *crossed fingers*). How many can you name?

TABLE TALK

Name one thing you could brag about, if you were the bragging type.

TABLE TALK

Name one thing you could brag about, if you were the bragging type.

TABLE TALK

Why do you think the legendary vampire Dracula is kept at bay by holding up a cross?

TABLE TALK

Why do you think the legendary vampire Dracula is kept at bay by holding up a cross?

TABLE TALK

How do you define the word *theologian*?

TABLE TALK

How do you define the word *theologian*?

Photocopy this page on plain paper or card stock, then cut on the dotted lines.
Place a set of four cards on each table for Table Talk.

The Lutheran Course II Leader Book, copyright © 2007 Augsburg Fortress.
May be reproduced for local use.

Session 2

TABLE TALK

What (if anything) did you choose to have for breakfast this morning? *Why* did you choose this?

TABLE TALK

What (if anything) did you choose to have for breakfast this morning? *Why* did you choose this?

TABLE TALK

Form a sentence using the word *will* at least three times (for example, "What will Will will to Will Jr.?" or "Your will will will differently than my will will will").

TABLE TALK

Form a sentence using the word *will* at least three times (for example, "What will Will will to Will Jr.?" or "Your will will will differently than my will will will").

TABLE TALK

List some things you did not choose (when you were born, where you were born, to whom you were born, your DNA, your kindergarten teacher, that broken arm in eighth grade, falling in love, and so forth).

TABLE TALK

List some things you did not choose (when you were born, where you were born, to whom you were born, your DNA, your kindergarten teacher, that broken arm in eighth grade, falling in love, and so forth).

TABLE TALK

In five words or less, define *sin*.

TABLE TALK

In five words or less, define *sin*.

Photocopy this page on plain paper or card stock, then cut on the dotted lines.
Place a set of four cards on each table for Table Talk.

The Lutheran Course II Leader Book, copyright © 2007 Augsburg Fortress.
May be reproduced for local use.

Session 3

TABLE TALK

Is there such a thing as a free lunch?

TABLE TALK

Is there such a thing as a free lunch?

TABLE TALK

What is the most gracious thing someone did to (or for) you this past week? What is the most gracious thing you did for someone else (if you don't say so yourself)?

TABLE TALK

What is the most gracious thing someone did to (or for) you this past week? What is the most gracious thing you did for someone else (if you don't say so yourself)?

TABLE TALK

Grace. Forgiveness. Faith. Promise. Hope. Love. Charity. Rebirth. Which of these are nice names for a baby? Which are basic biblical concepts?

TABLE TALK

Grace. Forgiveness. Faith. Promise. Hope. Love. Charity. Rebirth. Which of these are nice names for a baby? Which are basic biblical concepts?

TABLE TALK

Name somebody you know who has a strong faith.

TABLE TALK

Name somebody you know who has a strong faith.

Photocopy this page on plain paper or card stock, then cut on the dotted lines.
Place a set of four cards on each table for Table Talk.

The Lutheran Course II Leader Book, copyright © 2007 Augsburg Fortress.
May be reproduced for local use.

Session 3 Skit

Scene: A father, mother, daughter, and son are seated around a table.

MOM:	Your father and I just wanted to let you both know how much we love you.
DAD:	Yes, we really are quite fond of you.
BRO:	Gee, that's great, Mom, Dad.
SIS:	Yes, lovely. But . . .
BRO:	But Sis and I were thinking about how much you love us and all, and . . .
SIS:	And we were just wondering: what can we do to earn your love?
MOM & DAD:	What?
SIS:	For years you've told us over and over that you love us. But, frankly, we find this hard to believe. We don't think we deserve your love, so Bro and I would like to do some good works to be worthy of your great love for us.
DAD:	Errr . . .
MOM:	But, kids, you don't have to *do anything* for us to love you. You know that.
BRO:	Mother, Mother, Mother. Don't be so naïve. Who ever heard of getting something for nothing? *Of course* we have to do *something* to earn the right to be part of this family.
DAD:	What are you talking about? You *are* part of this family, whether you like it or not.
SIS:	That may be true. But for you to continue to love and bless us, there must be something we have to do to prove to you we are worthy of your love and blessing.
MOM:	This is crazy talk! We have loved you and blessed you since the day you were born—we've given you food, a comfortable home, lots of affection, guidance, and more! You've never had to prove you're worthy of any of this. We've given you these things freely, out of love—you've never had to do anything to earn our blessing! We live our lives for you, and you know we'd lay down our lives for you as well.

The Lutheran Course II Leader Book, copyright © 2007 Augsburg Fortress.
May be reproduced for local use.

Bro: Okay, okay. You've made your point. But certainly, there must be something else we can do. What if we declared that we *believe* in you?

Sis: Great idea, Bro. Mom, Dad, we believe that you exist.

Mom: Of course we exist! Who do you think gave you life? Who do you think brought you into this world? Who do you think raised you?

Sis: What we mean is that we have faith in you—you know: we trust in you.

Mom: Well, that's good to know. After all we've done for you: changing diapers, drying tears, tolerating your tantrums, forgiving your disobedience, giving you all good things! I should hope you've developed a bit of trust in us!

Bro: No, Mom, you're missing the point. Trusting in you is what *we do* to earn your love and blessing. Your patient forbearance and self-sacrifice have nothing to do with the fact that we trust in you. Instead, we've mustered up this trust all on our own.

Dad: *(after a pause)* Let's try this again—from the beginning.

Mom & Dad: We love you . . .

Session 4

TABLE TALK Which of the Ten Commandments do you think is easiest to keep? (You'll find the Commandments in Exodus 20 and Deuteronomy 5.)	**TABLE TALK** Which of the Ten Commandments do you think is easiest to keep? (You'll find the Commandments in Exodus 20 and Deuteronomy 5.)
TABLE TALK How many of the Ten Commandments are also written into criminal law where you live?	**TABLE TALK** How many of the Ten Commandments are also written into criminal law where you live?
TABLE TALK In 10 words or less, define *hypocrisy*. Next, give an example of hypocrisy.	**TABLE TALK** In 10 words or less, define *hypocrisy*. Next, give an example of hypocrisy.
TABLE TALK What does it mean to have a "left brain" and a "right brain"? What does it mean to be "of two minds"?	**TABLE TALK** What does it mean to have a "left brain" and a "right brain"? What does it mean to be "of two minds"?

Photocopy this page on plain paper or card stock, then cut on the dotted lines.
Place a set of four cards on each table for Table Talk.

The Lutheran Course II Leader Book, copyright © 2007 Augsburg Fortress.
May be reproduced for local use.

Session 5

TABLE TALK	TABLE TALK
Is there such a thing as a stupid question?	Is there such a thing as a stupid question?

TABLE TALK	TABLE TALK
Have you ever watched *Mister Rogers' Neighborhood*? Did you enjoy it? (Come on, you can admit it.)	Have you ever watched *Mister Rogers' Neighborhood*? Did you enjoy it? (Come on, you can admit it.)

TABLE TALK	TABLE TALK
Describe the best neighbors you've known.	Describe the best neighbors you've known.

TABLE TALK	TABLE TALK
Is it ever a bad idea to be a "good Samaritan"?	Is it ever a bad idea to be a "good Samaritan"?

Photocopy this page on plain paper or card stock, then cut on the dotted lines.
Place a set of four cards on each table for Table Talk.

The Lutheran Course II Leader Book, copyright © 2007 Augsburg Fortress.
May be reproduced for local use.

Session 6

TABLE TALK

Do you know anyone who is ambidextrous (equally capable from the left or right side)?

TABLE TALK

Do you know anyone who is ambidextrous (equally capable from the left or right side)?

TABLE TALK

Are you "left-brained" (more logical and detail oriented) or "right-brained" (more creative and big-picture oriented)?

TABLE TALK

Are you "left-brained" (more logical and detail oriented) or "right-brained" (more creative and big-picture oriented)?

TABLE TALK

Summarize a fairy tale or movie that involves a king and/or a queen.

TABLE TALK

Summarize a fairy tale or movie that involves a king and/or a queen.

TABLE TALK

What ruler or leader are you most like? (This can be a fictional character, historical figure, or present-day person.)

TABLE TALK

What ruler or leader are you most like? (This can be a fictional character, historical figure, or present-day person.)

Photocopy this page on plain paper or card stock, then cut on the dotted lines.
Place a set of four cards on each table for Table Talk.

The Lutheran Course II Leader Book, copyright © 2007 Augsburg Fortress.
May be reproduced for local use.

Session 7

TABLE TALK	TABLE TALK
Name an exotic vacation destination.	Name an exotic vacation destination.
TABLE TALK	**TABLE TALK**
Give an example of a tough job (but someone's gotta do it).	Give an example of a tough job (but someone's gotta do it).
TABLE TALK	**TABLE TALK**
Give an example of a spiritual calling.	Give an example of a spiritual calling.
TABLE TALK	**TABLE TALK**
Define *vocation* (and while you're at it, define *vacation*).	Define *vocation* (and while you're at it, define *vacation*).

Photocopy this page on plain paper or card stock, then cut on the dotted lines.
Place a set of four cards on each table for Table Talk.

The Lutheran Course II Leader Book, copyright © 2007 Augsburg Fortress.
May be reproduced for local use.

Session 7

Thank you for taking *The Lutheran Course II*. Please take a few minutes to complete this survey. Your feedback will be used to improve future sessions of the course.

1. *The Lutheran Course II* connected with my daily life.

    Strongly Agree   Agree   Disagree   Strongly Disagree

2. The course helped build positive relationships within my group.

    Strongly Agree   Agree   Disagree   Strongly Disagree

3. My preparation for the sessions took a reasonable amount of time.

    Strongly Agree   Agree   Disagree   Strongly Disagree

4. I will recommend *The Lutheran Course II* to others.

    Strongly Agree   Agree   Disagree   Strongly Disagree

5. I would like to help with future sessions of *The Lutheran Course II* in the following ways. (If interested, check all that apply and provide your name and contact information below.)
    - ○ Assisting with child care
    - ○ Helping with meals or refreshments
    - ○ Promoting the course
    - ○ Leading music
    - ○ Facilitating group discussion
    - ○ Other: _____

6. Describe the strengths of this course:

7. Describe ways the course could be improved:

8. Any additional comments:

Name _____   Phone _____

E-mail _____

Course Evaluation Form: Photocopy for use in the large group.
The Lutheran Course II Leader Book, copyright © 2007 Augsburg Fortress. May be reproduced for local use.

www.ingramcontent.com/pod-product-compliance
Lightning Source LLC
Chambersburg PA
CBHW082244300426
44110CB00036B/2443